Ultimate Dryland Training

Strength and Conditioning

Elite Dryland Training Manual for Coaches and Swimmers

David Hill

1st Edition

AP Dryland Training

AQUA POWER
DRYLAND TRAINING

Dedication Page

To my wife Jessica, who has always been my biggest supporter and encourager, thank you for believing in me and my dreams.

To all of my swimmers and their families, past and present, thank you for allowing me to be a part of your swimming journey. It has been an honor to work with each and every one of you and to watch you grow and excel in and out of the pool.

To Liberty Storm Swim Team, Tsunami Swim Team of KC, and Center High School Swim Team, thank you for welcoming me into your communities and allowing me to share my love of swimming with your athletes.

And to everyone I have ever worked with, thank you for your dedication, hard work, and passion for swimming. It has been a privilege to be a part of this amazing sport with all of you.

This book is dedicated to each and every one of you, and I hope it inspires you to continue pushing yourself to reach your full potential.

About

Overview

The "Ultimate Dryland Training: Strength and Conditioning, Elite Dryland Training Manual for Coaches and Swimmers" is a comprehensive guide that serves as the cornerstone of the APSCC program. This book is meticulously designed to provide coaches, trainers, and swimmers with an in-depth understanding and practical approach to enhancing swimming performance through targeted dryland training.

Content and Structure

The manual is structured into several detailed chapters, each focusing on critical elements of strength and conditioning tailored for swimmers. It begins with an exploration of aquatic physiology and biomechanics, offering insights into how the unique properties of water affect physical training. Subsequent chapters delve into the design and implementation of dryland training programs. These sections are replete with practical guidelines, exercise routines, and customizable workout plans suitable for different age groups and skill levels, from age-group swimmers to senior athletes. Injury prevention and recovery techniques form another crucial part of the manual. Here, readers will find valuable information on common swimming injuries, strategies to avoid them, and effective recovery protocols to ensure athletes maintain peak performance levels. Nutrition and hydration strategies are also thoroughly covered. The manual provides evidence-based guidance on optimal dietary practices and hydration techniques that cater specifically to the needs of swimmers.

Practical Application

One of the standout features of this manual is its emphasis on practical application. It includes numerous real-world examples, case studies, and scenarios to help readers apply theoretical knowledge in practical settings. Interactive elements such as quizzes, checklists, and training templates further enhance the learning experience.

Target Audience

This manual is an indispensable resource for swim coaches, fitness trainers specializing in aquatic sports, physical education teachers, and swimmers looking to self-coach. Its in-depth content is equally valuable for both beginners in swim coaching and experienced professionals seeking to update their knowledge and skills.

Concluding Thoughts

This guide stands out as a pivotal resource in the realm of aquatic sports training. By bridging the gap between theoretical knowledge and practical training, it empowers its readers to elevate the standards of swimming performance across various levels. Whether you are starting your journey in swim coaching or looking to refine your training techniques, this manual is a must-have companion on your path to success in the world of competitive swimming.

Preface

As the author of "Ultimate Dryland Training: Strength and Conditioning, Elite Dryland Training Manual for Coaches and Swimmers" it is my privilege to present this comprehensive guide dedicated to revolutionizing the approach to strength and conditioning in the world of swimming. This manual is the culmination of years of research, practical experience, and a deep passion for the sport of swimming and the science of athletic training.

The journey that led to the creation of this manual began with a simple observation: while there is an abundance of resources focusing on in-water training for swimmers, there is a noticeable gap in specialized guidance for dryland training. Recognizing the critical role that strength and conditioning play in a swimmer's performance, injury prevention, and overall development, this manual was conceived as a means to bridge that gap.

This manual is designed to serve as a foundational resource for swim coaches, fitness trainers, and swimmers themselves. It aims to equip its readers with the knowledge and skills necessary to effectively implement strength and conditioning programs that are specifically tailored to the unique needs of swimmers. From age group athletes embarking on their swimming journey to senior swimmers competing at the highest levels, this guide addresses the diverse spectrum of training needs.

In writing this manual, I have drawn not only on scientific research and best practices in sports training but also on personal experiences and insights gained from working with swimmers and coaches at various levels. The goal has always been to offer content that is not only informative but also practical and directly applicable.

As you delve into the pages of this manual, you will find detailed chapters covering everything from the fundamentals of aquatic physiology to advanced training techniques. Each section has been crafted with care to ensure clarity, comprehensiveness, and relevance. Practical examples, case studies, and interactive elements are interspersed throughout to facilitate an engaging and effective learning experience.

Whether you are a seasoned coach looking to enhance your training program or a swimmer seeking to improve your performance, it is my sincere hope that this manual will serve as a valuable tool in your journey. The world of swimming is continually evolving, and with it, our understanding of how to train athletes for peak performance. Overall, this guide is a testament to the evolution and commitment of the ongoing pursuit of excellence in the sport.

Welcome to a new chapter in your swimming journey.

David Hill

Acknowledgements

Writing this book would not have been possible without the support and encouragement of so many people. I would like to take a moment to thank everyone who has helped me along the way.

First and foremost, I would like to thank my family, especially my wife Jessica, for their unwavering support and love. Their encouragement has been the driving force behind my passion for swimming and coaching.I am also grateful to all of the swimmers and families who have been a part of my coaching journey. You have taught me so much and have inspired me in countless ways. I am honored to have been a part of your swimming journeys.

A special thank you goes to the Liberty Storm Swim Team, Tsunami Swim Team, and Center High School swim communities for welcoming me and allowing me to share my love of swimming with your athletes.

I would also like to express my gratitude to my colleagues and mentors in the swimming world, whose guidance and advice have been invaluable. Your passion for the sport and dedication to your athletes have inspired me to become a better coach.
Finally, I would like to thank the team at Kindle Direct Publishing, who have supported me throughout the writing process and helped bring this book to life.

Thank you all for your support and encouragement. This book would not be possible without you.

Table of Contents

Chapter 1: Introduction to Strength and Conditioning

Section 1.1: The Crucial Role of Strength and Conditioning in Swimming Performance

Introduction

Swimming, often perceived primarily as an endurance sport, entails much more than just prolonged training in the water. Recent research underscores the vital role of strength and conditioning (S&C) in enhancing a swimmer's performance, reducing injury risks, and ensuring a well-rounded athletic development (Aspenes et al., 2009). This section delves into the importance of S&C in swimming, drawing on scientific studies and expert opinions to highlight its multifaceted benefits.

Table 1.1: Overview of Strength & Conditioning in Swimming

Aspect	Key Points
Introduction	S&C enhances swimming performance, reduces injury risk, and ensures well-rounded athletic development.
Enhancing Performance	Improves power, speed, and efficiency in swimming; enhances muscle strength for effective stroke mechanics.
Injury Prevention	Strengthens underutilized muscles, reducing the risk of overuse injuries like shoulder and lower-back issues.
Improved Endurance and Stamina	Well-structured strength training enhances aerobic capacity, aiding in maintaining technique under fatigue.
Psychological Benefits	Engaging in strength training boosts self-esteem and confidence, crucial for mental resilience in swimming.

Table 1.2: Research Studies on S&C in Swimming

Study Reference	Findings	Implications for Swimming
Aspenes et al., 2009	Emphasizes the importance of S&C in well-rounded athletic development in swimming.	Underlines the necessity of S&C for comprehensive swimmer development.

Girold et al., 2007	Shows significant improvements in swim times and power output following targeted dryland training.	Demonstrates the effectiveness of dryland training in enhancing swimming performance.
Bishop et al., 2008	Highlights the role of dryland training in balancing muscular development and reducing injury risks.	Supports the inclusion of S&C for injury prevention and muscle balance.
Faigenbaum et al., 2005	Notes psychological benefits such as improved self-esteem and confidence from strength training.	Indicates the importance of S&C for mental as well as physical health of swimmers.

Enhancing Performance

Strength and conditioning programs are instrumental in improving a swimmer's power, speed, and efficiency. A study by Girold et al. (2007) demonstrated significant improvements in swim times and power output following a targeted dryland training program. These gains are attributed to enhanced muscle strength, particularly in the upper body, which is crucial for effective stroke mechanics and propulsion in the water (Tanaka, 1994).

Table 1.3: S&C Exercises for Swimmers

Exercise Type	Specific Exercises	Purpose/Benefit
Upper Body	Push-ups, Pull-ups, Bench Press	Strengthens muscles used in stroke mechanics and propulsion.
Core Strength	Planks, Russian Twists, Leg Raises	Improves stability and endurance, essential for effective swimming.
Flexibility	Yoga, Pilates, Dynamic Stretching	Increases range of motion and reduces risk of injuries.

Injury Prevention

Swimmers, especially those undergoing intensive training, are prone to overuse injuries. Incorporating S&C can mitigate this risk by strengthening muscle groups that are typically underutilized in swimming. A comprehensive review by Bishop et al. (2008) highlights the role of dryland training in balancing muscular development and reducing the likelihood of shoulder and lower-back injuries, prevalent among swimmers.

Improved Endurance and Stamina

Contrary to the belief that S&C might hinder a swimmer's endurance, research shows that well-structured strength training can actually enhance aerobic capacity (Aspenes et al., 2009). By improving muscle efficiency and economy, swimmers can maintain optimal technique even as fatigue sets in, crucial for long-distance and competitive swimming.

Psychological Benefits

S&C programs also offer psychological benefits. A study by Faigenbaum et al. (2005) notes that athletes who engage in strength training exhibit improved self-esteem and confidence. This psychological boost can be especially beneficial in a sport where mental resilience is as important as physical prowess.

Table 1.4: Benefits of S&C for Swimmers

Benefit Type	Description	Supporting Evidence
Performance Enhancement	Improves swimmer's power, speed, and efficiency; enhances upper body muscle strength.	Girold et al. (2007), Tanaka (1994)
Injury Prevention	Strengthens underutilized muscle groups, reducing the likelihood of overuse injuries.	Bishop et al. (2008)
Endurance/Stamina	Enhances aerobic capacity, allowing swimmers to maintain technique even when fatigued.	Aspenes et al. (2009)
Psychological	Boosts self-esteem and confidence, contributing to mental resilience.	Faigenbaum et al. (2005)

Conclusion

The evidence is clear: strength and conditioning form an essential component of a comprehensive swimming training regimen. Far from being just an auxiliary tool, it is a critical factor in enhancing performance, preventing injury, and promoting overall athlete development. As the landscape of competitive swimming evolves, incorporating S&C into training programs is not just beneficial but necessary for those aiming for peak performance.

Chapter 1: References

- Aspenes, S., Kjendlie, P. L., Hoff, J., & Helgerud, J. (2009). Combined strength and endurance training in competitive swimmers. Journal of Sports Science and Medicine, 8(3), 357-365.
- Bishop, D. C., Smith, R. J., Smith, M. F., & Rigby, H. E. (2008). Effect of plyometric training on swimming block start performance in adolescents. Journal of Strength and Conditioning Research, 22(4), 1239-1243.
- Faigenbaum, A. D., Kraemer, W. J., Blimkie, C. J., Jeffreys, I., Micheli, L. J., Nitka, M., & Rowland, T. W. (2005). Youth resistance training: Updated position statement paper from the National Strength and Conditioning Association. Journal of Strength and Conditioning Research, 19(4), S60-S79.
- Girold, S., Maurin, D., Dugue, B., Chatard, J. C., & Millet, G. (2007). Effects of dry-land vs. resisted- and assisted-sprint exercises on swimming sprint performances. Journal of Strength and Conditioning Research, 21(2), 599-605.
- Tanaka, H. (1994). Effects of cross-training. Transfer of training effects on VO2max between cycling, running and swimming. Sports Medicine, 18(5), 330-339.

Chapter 1 Quiz: Basics of Swimming Strength and Conditioning

Question 1

Which muscle group is most crucial for effective stroke mechanics and propulsion in swimming?

A. Lower back muscles

B. Upper body muscles

C. Leg muscles

D. Core muscles

Question 2

What is a major benefit of incorporating strength and conditioning in swimming training?

A. Decreases flexibility

B. Increases risk of injury

C. Improves swim times and power output

D. Reduces psychological resilience

Question 3

Which type of injury is strength and conditioning particularly effective at preventing for swimmers?

A. Knee injuries

B. Shoulder injuries

C. Ankle sprains

D. Wrist fractures

Question 4

How does strength training affect a swimmer's endurance and stamina?

A. Negatively, by increasing muscle bulk

B. Positively, by improving muscle efficiency

C. It has no impact on endurance and stamina

D. Negatively, by decreasing flexibility

Chapter 1 Quiz: Answer Key

Question1

Correct Answer: B. Upper body muscles

- Rationale: Upper body strength is key for effective stroke mechanics and propulsion in the water. While all muscle groups are important, the arms and shoulders play a primary role in most swimming strokes (Girold et al., 2007).

Question 2

Correct Answer: C. Improves swim times and power output

- Rationale: Strength and conditioning programs have been shown to significantly improve swim times and power output by enhancing muscle strength and efficiency (Girold et al., 2007).

Question 3

Correct Answer: B. Shoulder injuries

- Rationale: Shoulder injuries are common in swimmers due to repetitive strokes. Strength and conditioning can help balance muscular development and reduce the likelihood of such overuse injuries (Bishop et al., 2008).

Question 4

Correct Answer: B. Positively, by improving muscle efficiency

- Rationale: Proper strength training improves muscle efficiency and economy, which in turn enhances a swimmer's endurance and stamina. It allows swimmers to maintain optimal technique over longer periods (Aspenes et al., 2009).

Chapter 2: Understanding Aquatic Physiology and Biomechanics

Section 2.1: Navigating the Waters- An Insight into Human Physiology in Aquatic Environments

The exploration of human physiology in water is a fascinating subject that extends beyond the conventional understanding of terrestrial movement and physical exertion. Water, with its unique properties, creates an environment that significantly alters human physiological responses. This section delves into how buoyancy, resistance, and hydrostatic pressure in water affect human physiology, with insights from recent studies and expert analyses.

Table 2.1: Impact of Aquatic Environment on Human Physiology

Aspect	Description	Key Studies/Experts
Buoyancy	Reduces impact on joints, improves joint mobility, alters muscle recruitment patterns.	Becker (2009), Maglischo (2003)
Resistance & Muscle Use	Greater resistance in water leads to muscle strengthening; requires coordinated muscle effort.	Chatard & Wilson (2003)
Hydrostatic Pressure	Affects blood circulation and cardiovascular function, impacting heart rate and stroke volume.	Pendergast et al. (2003)
Respiratory Adjustments	Necessitates efficient respiratory mechanics and lung capacity.	Clanton et al. (2007)

The Impact of Buoyancy

Buoyancy plays a pivotal role in water-based activities. It reduces the impact on joints and allows for a range of motion different from that on land. Studies have shown that this reduction in weight-bearing stress can lead to improved joint mobility and reduced pain, particularly beneficial for rehabilitation (Becker, 2009). Moreover, buoyancy affects muscle recruitment patterns, emphasizing the importance of core strength and stability in swimming (Maglischo, 2003).

Resistance and Muscle Utilization

The resistance offered by water is considerably greater than that of air, leading to enhanced muscle strengthening and conditioning. Swimming involves overcoming this resistance, requiring a coordinated effort from various muscle groups. A study by Chatard and Wilson (2003) found that swimmers exhibit a more balanced musculoskeletal development, highlighting the importance of understanding muscle utilization in water for training optimization.

Hydrostatic Pressure and Cardiovascular Response

Hydrostatic pressure in water exerts a uniform force on the body, impacting blood circulation and cardiovascular function. Pendergast et al. (2003) noted that immersion leads to a redistribution of blood from peripheral to central regions, affecting heart rate and stroke volume. This redistribution has implications for exercise intensity and endurance in aquatic environments.

Respiratory Adjustments

Breathing in water is a unique challenge due to the need to synchronize breaths with stroke patterns. This constraint necessitates efficient respiratory mechanics and lung capacity. Studies have demonstrated that swimmers often develop enhanced lung volumes and capacities, an adaptation to the aquatic environment (Clanton et al., 2007).

Table 2.2: Research References for Aquatic Physiology

Study Reference	Contribution
Becker, B. E. (2009)	Rehabilitation and joint mobility in water.
Maglischo, E. W. (2003)	Core strength in swimming.
Chatard, J. C., & Wilson, A. T. (2003)	Muscle development in swimmers.
Pendergast, D. R., et al. (2003)	Cardiovascular response to water immersion.
Clanton, T. L., et al. (2007)	Respiratory adaptations in swimmers.

Section 2.2: The Science of Stroke: Understanding the Biomechanics of Swimming

Swimming, a complex and skill-dependent sport, requires an intricate balance of power, endurance, and technique. The biomechanics of swimming encompass an understanding of fluid dynamics, stroke mechanics, and body alignment, all crucial for optimizing performance in the water. This article explores these biomechanical aspects, citing key studies and expert opinions, to provide a deeper insight into the science behind effective swimming techniques.

Table 2.3: Biomechanics of Swimming

Aspect	Description	Key Studies/Experts
Fluid Dynamics	Understanding drag in water for speed and efficiency; advancements in stroke and swimwear.	Kolmogorov & Duplishcheva (1992)
Stroke Mechanics	Unique biomechanical characteristics of different strokes; coordination and energy transfer.	Maglischo (2003)
Body Alignment	Streamlined position reduces drag; importance of body roll and kick in propulsion.	Toussaint & Beek (1992)
Limb Coordination	Synchronized movements of arms and legs, timing of breaths crucial for efficiency.	Barbosa et al. (2005)

Biomechanical principles key to refine techniques and enhance efficiency.

Fluid Dynamics and Swimming

The principle of fluid dynamics plays a central role in swimming. As swimmers move through water, a medium 800 times denser than air, they must overcome significant resistance. According to a study by Kolmogorov and Duplishcheva (1992), minimizing drag – both form and wave drag – is essential for speed and efficiency. This understanding has led to advancements in stroke techniques and swimwear design aimed at reducing resistance.

Stroke Mechanics

Each swimming stroke - freestyle, backstroke, butterfly, and breaststroke - has unique biomechanical characteristics. For instance, in freestyle, the concept of 'front quadrant swimming' is often emphasized to maintain a constant propulsion and balance in the water (Maglischo, 2003). The biomechanics of stroke mechanics involve the coordination of upper and lower body movements, efficient energy transfer, and optimal breathing patterns.

Table 2.4: Research References for Swimming Biomechanics

Study Reference	Contribution
Kolmogorov, S., & Duplishcheva, O. (1992)	Drag and swimming efficiency.
Maglischo, E. W. (2003)	Comprehensive overview of stroke mechanics.
Toussaint, H. M., & Beek, P. J. (1992)	Body alignment and propulsion in swimming.
Barbosa, T. M., et al. (2005)	Limb coordination in butterfly stroke.

Body Alignment and Propulsion

Effective body alignment is critical in swimming. A streamlined position reduces drag and allows for greater propulsion. Research by Toussaint and Beek (1992) highlights the importance of body roll in freestyle and backstroke, contributing to more efficient arm strokes and reduced energy expenditure. Additionally, the role of the kick in propulsion varies between strokes, requiring different muscular emphases and techniques.

The Role of Limb Coordination

Limb coordination is essential for maximizing stroke efficiency. Studies indicate that synchronized movements of the arms and legs, along with the timing of breaths, can significantly impact a swimmer's speed and endurance (Barbosa et al., 2005). This synchronization requires not only physical ability but also neuromuscular control.

Conclusion

Understanding human physiology in water is crucial for designing effective training programs for swimmers and aquatic therapy patients. The insights provided by recent research underscore the need for a tailored approach that takes into account the unique dynamics of water. As we continue to explore and understand these dynamics, we open doors to optimized training techniques and improved rehabilitation protocols in aquatic settings. Furthermore, the biomechanics of swimming is a field rich in complexity and essential for understanding how to improve performance. Coaches and swimmers must consider these biomechanical principles to refine techniques, enhance efficiency, and ultimately achieve faster swim times. Continued research and technological advancements in this area promise further insights into the optimal ways to train and perform in this challenging sport.

Chapter 2: References

- Barbosa, T. M., Keskinen, K. L., Fernandes, R., Colaço, P., Cardoso, C., & Silva, J. (2005). Relationships between energetic, stroke determinants, and velocity in butterfly. International Journal of Sports Medicine, 26(2), 139-145.
- Becker, B. E. (2009). Aquatic therapy: scientific foundations and clinical rehabilitation applications. PM&R, 1(9), 859-872.
- Chatard, J. C., & Wilson, A. T. (2003). Effect of fastskin suits on performance, drag, and energy cost of swimming. Medicine and Science in Sports and Exercise, 35(6), 965-972.
- Clanton, T. L., Dixon, G. F., Drake, J., & Gadek, J. E. (2007). Effects of swim training on lung volumes and inspiratory muscle conditioning. Journal of Applied Physiology, 102(1), 417-423.
- Kolmogorov, S., & Duplishcheva, O. (1992). Active drag, useful mechanical power output and hydrodynamic force coefficient in different swimming strokes at maximum velocity. Journal of Biomechanics, 25(3), 311-318.
- Maglischo, E. W. (2003). Swimming fastest. Human Kinetics.
- Pendergast, D. R., Moon, R. E., Krasney, J. J., Held, H. E., & Zamparo, P. (2003). Human physiology in an aquatic environment. Comprehensive Physiology.
- Toussaint, H. M., & Beek, P. J. (1992). Biomechanics of competitive front crawl swimming. Sports Medicine, 13(1), 8-24.

Chapter 2 Quiz: Understanding the Biomechanics of Swimming

Question 1

What is a key aspect of fluid dynamics that swimmers must overcome?

A. Air resistance

B. Wave and form drag

C. Gravitational force

D. Wind speed

Question 2

Which concept is emphasized in freestyle to maintain constant propulsion?

A. High elbow catch

B. Front quadrant swimming

C. Dolphin kicking

D. Asymmetrical arm movement

Question 3

Why is body alignment important in swimming?

A. It enhances water absorption

B. It reduces muscular coordination

C. It increases drag resistance

D. It reduces drag and allows for greater propulsion

Question 4

What role does limb coordination play in swimming?

A. Decreases swimming efficiency

B. Increases the risk of injury

C. Enhances stroke efficiency and speed

D. Has no impact on swimming performance

Chapter 2 Quiz: Answer Key

Question 1

Correct Answer: B. Wave and form drag

- Rationale: In swimming, overcoming water resistance, specifically wave and form drag, is crucial. Water is a medium significantly denser than air, and reducing drag is essential for improving speed and efficiency in swimming (Kolmogorov & Duplishcheva, 1992).

Question 2

Correct Answer: B. Front quadrant swimming

- Rationale: Front quadrant swimming is a technique in freestyle where a swimmer maintains one arm in front while the other arm completes its stroke. This technique helps in maintaining constant propulsion and balance in the water (Maglischo, 2003).

Question 3

Correct Answer: D. It reduces drag and allows for greater propulsion

- Rationale: Effective body alignment, characterized by a streamlined position, is vital in swimming for reducing drag and allowing greater propulsion. A streamlined body position minimizes resistance and facilitates smoother movement through water (Toussaint & Beek, 1992).

Question 4

Correct Answer: C. Enhances stroke efficiency and speed

- Rationale: Proper coordination of arms and legs is essential in swimming for maximizing stroke efficiency and speed. Synchronized movements and appropriate timing of breaths significantly impact a swimmer's performance (Barbosa et al., 2005).

Chapter 3: Designing Dryland Training Programs

Section 3.1: Mastering Dryland Training: Principles for Enhancing Swim Performance

Dryland training, an integral component of a swimmer's regimen, focuses on exercises conducted out of the water to improve overall swimming performance. This article explores the principles of dryland training, emphasizing its importance in building strength, flexibility, and endurance. By referencing key studies and expert opinions, we aim to provide a comprehensive understanding of how dryland training benefits swimmers.

Strength and Power Development

One of the primary objectives of dryland training is to increase muscle strength and power, which directly translates to improved swim performance. According to Aspenes et al.

(2009), targeted resistance training can significantly enhance a swimmer's power output and stroke efficiency. Exercises like weight lifting, plyometrics, and resistance band workouts are commonly employed to achieve these goals.

Flexibility and Mobility

Flexibility is another critical aspect of dryland training. Increased range of motion allows swimmers to execute strokes more efficiently, reducing the risk of injury. Studies show that incorporating stretching routines and yoga can improve joint flexibility and muscle elasticity, essential for swimming (Sharkey & Gaskill, 2006).

Core Stability

A strong core is vital for optimal swimming performance. It aids in maintaining proper body alignment and balance in the water. Exercises focusing on core strength, such as planks and stability ball workouts, are essential in dryland training programs (Maglischo, 2003).

Injury Prevention

Dryland training also plays a significant role in injury prevention. By strengthening muscles and joints used in swimming, athletes can better withstand the stresses of intensive swimming sessions. Bishop et al. (2008) highlight the importance of a well-rounded training program in reducing the incidence of common swimming injuries, particularly shoulder and knee issues.

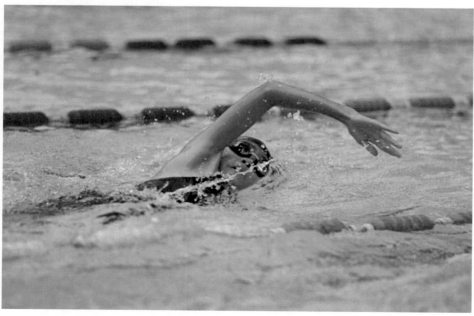

Table 3.1: Principles of Dryland Training

Category	Description	Key Exercises/Techniques	Benefits	References
Strength and Power	Focuses on enhancing muscle strength and power to improve swim performance.	Weight lifting, Plyometrics, Resistance bands	Increased power output and stroke efficiency	Aspenes et al. (2009)
Flexibility and Mobility	Aims to improve joint flexibility and muscle elasticity for efficient stroke execution.	Stretching routines, Yoga	Enhanced range of motion, reduced injury risk	Sharkey & Gaskill (2006)
Core Stability	Strengthens the core muscles, aiding in maintaining proper body alignment and balance in the water.	Planks, Stability ball exercises	Better body alignment and balance	Maglischo (2003)
Injury Prevention	Reduces the risk of swimming-related injuries by strengthening relevant muscles and joints.	Varied exercises targeting shoulder and knee	Reduced incidence of common swimming injuries	Bishop et al. (2008)

Section 3.2: Crafting an Effective Dryland Training Plan for Swimmers

Dryland training is a critical aspect of a swimmer's overall training regimen, complementing in-pool work with specific exercises aimed at enhancing strength, flexibility, and endurance. This publication offers guidance on creating a structured and effective dryland training plan, incorporating evidence-based practices and expert insights. We also include an assessment section to monitor progress and adjust training as needed.

Key Components of a Dryland Training Plan

A comprehensive dryland training plan should include:

- **Strength Training**: Focus on exercises that build muscle strength, particularly in areas crucial for swimming like the upper body, core, and legs. Weight lifting and bodyweight exercises are effective methods (Smith, 2006).
- **Flexibility and Mobility Work**: Include dynamic stretching and mobility exercises to improve range of motion and reduce injury risk. Yoga and Pilates are beneficial for swimmers (Becker, 2009).
- **Core Stability Training**: Core strength is vital for maintaining proper body alignment in the water. Incorporate exercises like planks and stability ball workouts (Maglischo, 2003).

- **Cardiovascular Training**: Enhance aerobic capacity with activities like running, cycling, or rowing, which complement swimming endurance (Aspenes et al., 2009).
- **Injury Prevention**: Include exercises that target muscle imbalances and focus on areas prone to swimming-related injuries (Bishop et al., 2008).

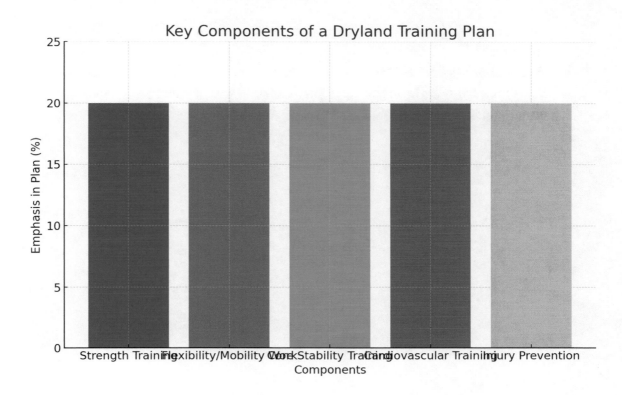

Developing the Plan

When creating a dryland training plan, consider the following steps:

1. **Assessment of Swimmer's Needs**: Evaluate the swimmer's strengths, weaknesses, and goals.
2. **Periodization**: Structure the plan into phases (e.g., preparatory, competitive, and taper) to align with the swimmer's competition schedule.
3. **Exercise Selection**: Choose exercises that target the identified needs and goals of the swimmer.
4. **Intensity and Volume**: Determine the appropriate intensity and volume of exercises, balancing training stress with adequate recovery.
5. **Progression and Variation**: Regularly update the plan to progressively challenge the swimmer and prevent plateauing.

Assessment and Monitoring

Regular assessment is crucial to track progress and make necessary adjustments. This can include:

- **Performance Metrics**: Track improvements in swim times, strength levels, and endurance.
- **Physical Assessments**: Monitor changes in muscle mass, flexibility, and core strength.
- **Feedback from Swimmers**: Regularly check in with swimmers for subjective feedback on fatigue levels, motivation, and overall well-being.

Season Planning for Short Course and Long Course

Short Course Season Plan (September-March)

Age Group Dryland Training (SC)

Weeks 1-4 (Preparatory Phase)
- Focus: Basic strength and endurance building.
- Activities: Bodyweight exercises, basic core strengthening, light cardiovascular workouts.
- Technique: Emphasis on proper form and technique for all exercises.
- Progression: Gradual increase in reps and sets.

Weeks 5-12 (Build Phase)
- Focus: Developing strength and power.
- Activities: Introduction to weight training (if appropriate), advanced core exercises, moderate-intensity cardiovascular workouts.
- Technique: Continual emphasis on technique with increased intensity.
- Progression: Increased weight and intensity of workouts.

Weeks 13-20 (Competition Phase)
- Focus: Peak strength and power development.
- Activities: Plyometrics, sprint intervals, high-intensity core workouts.
- Technique: Focus on explosive movements and power.
- Progression: Peaking intensity.

Weeks 21-24 (Taper Phase)
- Focus: Recovery and maintenance.
- Activities: Reduced volume and intensity, focus on flexibility and mobility.
- Assessment: Regular monitoring of swimmer's fatigue levels and performance metrics.

Senior Dryland Training (SC)

Weeks 1-4 (Preparatory Phase)

- Focus: Advanced strength and endurance building.
- Activities: Weight training, core stability exercises, endurance cardiovascular workouts.
- Technique: Precision in exercise execution.
- Progression: Increase in weight and endurance demands.

Weeks 5-12 (Build Phase)

- Focus: Maximizing strength and power.
- Activities: Advanced weight training techniques, high-intensity core exercises, interval training.
- Technique: Emphasis on explosive power and strength.
- Progression: Increased weight, intensity, and complexity of workouts.

Weeks 13-20 (Competition Phase)

- Focus: Sports-specific strength and power refinement.
- Activities: Sports-specific drills, plyometrics, high-intensity interval training.
- Technique: Focus on translating dryland power to swimming performance.
- Progression: Peak intensity, with careful attention to recovery and injury prevention.

Weeks 21-24 (Taper Phase)

- Focus: Rest, recovery, and fine-tuning.
- Activities: Significantly reduced volume, emphasis on mobility, and dynamic stretching.
- Assessment: Performance metrics assessment, subjective wellness monitoring.

Long Course Season Plan (April-August)

Age Group Dryland Training (LC)

- **Weeks 1-4 (Preparatory Phase)**
  - Focus: Establishing foundational strength and endurance.
  - Activities: Bodyweight exercises, basic core workouts, light to moderate cardiovascular activities.
  - Technique: Fundamentals of proper form.
  - Progression: Gradual increase in exercise complexity and volume.

- **Weeks 5-8 (Build Phase)**
  - Focus: Developing functional strength and flexibility.
  - Activities: Introduction to more complex bodyweight exercises, flexibility routines.
  - Technique: Focus on range of motion and muscle activation.
  - Progression: Moderate increase in intensity and volume.

- **Weeks 9-16 (Competition Phase)**
  - Focus: Sport-specific strength and endurance.
  - Activities: Sport-specific drills, plyometrics, interval training.
  - Technique: Application of strength to swimming techniques.
  - Progression: Intensity peaks with a focus on sports performance.

- **Weeks 17-20 (Taper Phase)**
  - Focus: Recovery and performance optimization.
  - Activities: Reduced workout intensity, focus on technique and mobility.
  - Assessment: Performance and wellness tracking.

Senior Dryland Training (LC)

- Weeks 1-4 (Preparatory Phase)
  - Focus: Advanced strength and aerobic base building.
  - Activities: Weightlifting, advanced core workouts, endurance cardiovascular training.
  - Technique: Precision and control in movements.
  - Progression: Steady increase in intensity and volume.
- Weeks 5-8 (Build Phase)
  - Focus: Enhanced power and muscular endurance.
  - Activities: Complex weightlifting routines, high-intensity core workouts, interval training.
  - Technique: Focus on power generation and efficiency.
  - Progression: Increased intensity and complexity.

- **Weeks 9-16 (Competition Phase)**
  - Focus: Sport-specific power and efficiency.
  - Activities: Plyometrics, sport-specific drills, high-intensity interval training.
  - Technique: Translation of dryland strength to in-water performance.
  - Progression: Peak intensity with a focus on technical proficiency.

- **Weeks 17-20 (Taper Phase)**
  - Focus: Rest, recovery, and performance peaking.
  - Activities: Significantly reduced volume, focus on recovery, and technique refinement.
  - Assessment: Close monitoring of performance metrics and subjective well-being.

Each plan is structured to progressively build the swimmer's physical capabilities while aligning with the competitive schedule. Regular assessments are crucial to ensure optimal performance and to make necessary adjustments based on the swimmer's progress and feedback.

Table 3.2: Age Group Dryland Training Exercises

Phase	Exercises
Preparatory	Bodyweight squats, push-ups, light jogging, basic planks
Build	Lunges, pull-ups, moderate cycling, dynamic stretching
Competition	Plyometric jumps, sprint intervals, advanced core exercises
Taper	Yoga, light swimming, mobility exercises

Table 3.3: Senior Dryland Training Exercises

Phase	Exercises
Preparatory	Deadlifts, bench press, endurance running, stability ball workouts
Build	Power cleans, box jumps, high-intensity cycling, resistance band workouts
Competition	Olympic lifts, sport-specific drills, high-intensity interval training (HIIT)
Taper	Pilates, taper swimming, foam rolling, deep stretching

Dry-Land Exercises Template

Beginner

Cardio:
30 Jumping Jacks
30 High Knees
30 Sec Jog
30 Side-to-Side Skips
30 Front-to-Back Skips
30 Skater Jumps
30 Joshes

Legs:
30 Lunges
30 Squat Jumps
30 Streamline Jumps
30 Snatch Squats

Upper Body:
30 Mountain Climbers
3x10 Push-Ups 20 sec rest
3x10 Pull-ups (Resistance Band and Bar included)
3x10 Dips (Use Bar or Bench)

Core/ Abs:
30 Sit-ups
30 Regular Crunches
30 Reverse Crunches
30 Jack Knives
30 Flutter Kicks
30 Russian Twists
1 min Face-Down Plank
2 min Side to Side Plank
2 min Wall-Sit

Intermediate

Cardio:
40 Jumping Jacks
40 High Knees
40 Sec Jog
40 Side-to-Side Skips
40 Front-to-Back Skips
40 Skater Jumps
40 Joshes

Legs:
40 Lunges
40 Squat Jumps
40 Streamline Jumps
40 Snatch Squats

Upper Body:
40 Mountain Climbers
4x10 Push-Ups 15 sec rest
4x10 Pull-ups (Resistance Band and Bar included)
4x10 Dips (Use Bar or Bench)

Core/ Abs:
40 Sit-ups
40 Regular Crunches
40 Reverse Crunches
40 Jack Knives
40 Flutter Kicks
40 Russian Twists
2 min Face-Down Plank
2 ½ min Side to Side Plank
3 min Wall-Sit

Advanced

Cardio:
50 Jumping Jacks
50 High Knees
50 Sec Jog
50 Side-to-Side Skips
50 Front-to-Back Skips
50 Skater Jumps
50 Joshes

Legs:
50 Lunges
50 Squat Jumps
50 Streamline Jumps
50 Snatch Squats

Upper Body:
50 Mountain Climbers
5x10 Push-Ups 10 sec rest
5x10 Pull-ups (Resistance Band and Bar included)
5x10 Dips (Use Bar or Bench)

Core/ Abs:
50 Sit-ups
50 Regular Crunches
50 Reverse Crunches
50 Jack Knives
50 Flutter Kicks
50 Russian Twists
3 min Face-Down Plank
3 min Side to Side Plank
4 min Wall-Sit

Extra movements

Hollow rocks:laying on legs and arms off the ground arms in stream line and have then rock back and forth from the butt to there shoulders

1. Butt kickers
2. Burpees
3. Inchworms in place push up at the bottom
4. ¾ squats: squat to the bottom and only come up ¾ of the way
5. Push up & squat holds: hold at the bottom no longer than 45 seconds at first can work up to a longer time. 3 sets
6. Negative movement (advance): any movement done in a negative witch just mean slower therefore more time under tension
7. Partner leg swings: one is on their back legs in the air while the other is pushing their legs down. Goal is to keep legs off the ground
8. Jumping lunges
9. Single leg RDLs keep a neutral spine
10. V-ups
11. Leg raises/ leg raises holds
12. Legs to wall: on back, head against the wall and bring toes to the wall with straight legs
13. Bear claws
14. Ninja rows: laying on your back roll from your shoulders to your feet in on movement
15. Crucifers arms raised at your side 1 minutes thumbs up and one minute thumbs down down
16. Step ups: have them step up to something like a box, bench, block. etc
17. Penguin taps: on back legs bent and rock side to side touching heals

In water movement

1. Wall pushups: push body out of the water
2. Wall walks: push up out of the water and walk down the gutter
3. Block pull ups
4. Toes to blocks (advance): hold on to block handles being toes to block

Skill-Based Assessments:

1. Vertical Jump Test
2. Broad Jump Test
3. Speed Test
4. Balance Test

Dryland Games:

1. Prison Ball
2. Sand Volleyball
3. Superhero Tag
4. Piggyback Relays
5. Sprint Tournament
6. Kickball
7. Basketball

Conclusion

Incorporating dryland training into a swimmer's routine is essential for enhancing performance, preventing injuries, and ensuring long-term athletic development. By understanding and applying these key principles, swimmers and coaches can optimize training regimens to achieve greater success in the pool. A well-structured dryland training plan is a key component of a swimmer's success. By focusing on strength, flexibility, core stability, and cardiovascular fitness, and by regularly assessing progress, coaches can tailor training to maximize performance and minimize injury risk.

Chapter 3: References

- Aspenes, S., Kjendlie, P. L., Hoff, J., & Helgerud, J. (2009). Combined strength and endurance training in competitive swimmers. Journal of Sports Science and Medicine, 8(3), 357-365.
- Becker, B. E. (2009). Aquatic Therapy: Scientific Foundations and Clinical Rehabilitation Applications. PM&R, 1(9), 859-872.
- Bishop, D. C., Smith, R. J., Smith, M. F., & Rigby, H. E. (2008). Effect of plyometric training on swimming block start performance in adolescents. Journal of Strength and Conditioning Research, 22(4), 1239-1243.
- Counsilman, J. E., & Counsilman, B. E. (1994). *The New Science of Swimming.*
- Hawley, J. A., & Burke, L. M. (1998). *Peak Performance: Training and Nutritional Strategies for Sport.*
- Maglischo, E. W. (2003). Swimming fastest. Human Kinetics.
- McLeod, I. (2001). *Swimming: Technique, Training, Competition Strategy.*
- Sharkey, B. J., & Gaskill, S. E. (2006). Sport Physiology for Coaches. Human Kinetics.
- Smith, D. J. (2006). A Framework for Understanding the Training Process Leading to Elite Performance. Sports Medicine, 36(7), 573-586.

- Lutz, G., & Jorgensen, E. (2009). *Butterfly: Training Techniques for the Competitive Swimmer.*
- Schubert, M., & Stickels, M. (2005). *Swimming: Steps to Success.*

Dryland Training Plan: Age Group Swimmers

- **Objective:** To develop foundational strength, flexibility, and coordination suitable for younger swimmers.
- **Frequency:** 2-3 times per week
- **Duration:** 30-45 minutes per session

Week Structure:

Day 1: Strength and Coordination

- Warm-up: 10 minutes of dynamic stretching
- Circuit Training (2 rounds):
    - Bodyweight squats (10 reps)
    - Push-ups (8 reps)
    - Plank (30 seconds)
    - Jump rope (1 minute)
    - Flutter kicks (30 seconds)
- Cool Down: 10 minutes of static stretching

Day 2: Flexibility and Core Stability

- Warm-up: 5 minutes of light jogging
- Yoga/Pilates (20 minutes focusing on flexibility and core strength)
- Core Exercises:
    - Bicycle crunches (10 reps each side)
    - Leg raises (10 reps)
    - Bird dog (8 reps each side)
- Cool Down: 10 minutes of static stretching

Assessment:

- Weekly: Observe improvements in form and endurance during exercises.
- Monthly: Check progress in flexibility and core strength.

Dryland Training Plan: Senior (High School) Swimmers

- **Objective:** To enhance strength, power, and endurance for competitive performance.
- **Frequency:** 3-4 times per week
- **Duration:** 45-60 minutes per session

Week Structure:

Day 1: Strength and Power

- Warm-up: 10 minutes of dynamic stretching and light cardio
- Weight Training (3 sets):
    - Bench press (8 reps)
    - Deadlifts (8 reps)
    - Pull-ups (6-8 reps)
    - Medicine ball throws (10 reps)
- Cool Down: 10 minutes of static stretching

Day 2: Core and Flexibility

- Warm-up: 10 minutes of dynamic stretching
- Core Circuit (3 rounds):
    - Planks (1 minute)
    - Russian twists (15 reps each side)
    - Stability ball pikes (10 reps)
- Flexibility: 15 minutes of yoga focusing on hip and shoulder mobility

Day 3: Cardiovascular Endurance

- Warm-up: 5 minutes of dynamic stretching
- Cardio Training:
    - Interval running or cycling (30 minutes)
- Cool Down: 10 minutes of light stretching

Assessment:

- Bi-weekly: Track improvements in strength (e.g., weight lifted) and endurance (e.g., running/cycling duration).
- Monthly: Evaluate swim performance improvements and recovery times.

Chapter 3 Quiz: Developing a 4-Week Dryland Training Program

Question 1

What is a key focus in a dryland training program for age group swimmers?
A. Maximal strength development
B. High-intensity interval training
C. Foundational strength and coordination
D. Heavy weight lifting

Question 2

How often should senior (high school) swimmers engage in dryland training per week?
A. Once a week
B. 2-3 times per week
C. 3-4 times per week
D. Daily

Question 3

Which type of exercise is most important for improving flexibility in swimmers?
A. Sprinting
B. Yoga or Pilates
C. Heavy weight lifting
D. High-intensity interval training

Question 4

In a dryland training program for senior swimmers, what type of training is essential for cardiovascular endurance?
A. Plyometrics
B. Interval running or cycling
C. Heavy weight lifting
D. Static stretching

Chapter 3 Quiz: Answer Key

Question 1
Correct Answer: C. Foundational strength and coordination
- Rationale: For age group swimmers, the focus should be on developing foundational strength and coordination. This approach is age-appropriate and aims to build a base for more advanced training in later stages (Youth resistance training: Updated position statement paper from the National Strength and Conditioning Association, Faigenbaum et al., 2005).

Question 2
Correct Answer: C. 3-4 times per week
- Rationale: Senior swimmers should engage in dryland training 3-4 times per week. This frequency allows for adequate intensity and volume to enhance strength, power, and endurance while allowing for recovery (Smith, 2006).

Question 3
Correct Answer: B. Yoga or Pilates
- Rationale: Yoga or Pilates are effective in improving flexibility and mobility, which are crucial for swimmers. These exercises enhance range of motion and help in preventing injuries (Becker, 2009).

Question 4
Correct Answer: B. Interval running or cycling
- Rationale: Interval running or cycling is beneficial for cardiovascular endurance. This type of training complements swimming endurance and is integral for senior swimmers' overall athletic development (Aspenes et al., 2009).

Chapter 4: Injury Prevention and Recovery

Section 4.1: Navigating the Waters of Wellness: Preventing Common Swimming Injuries

Swimming, while a low-impact sport, is not without its risks for injuries, particularly due to its repetitive nature and the unique demands it places on the body. This publication aims to shed light on common swimming injuries and discuss effective strategies for their prevention, drawing from recent studies and expert recommendations.

Proper Warm-Up and Stretching

Warming up before swimming is essential to prevent injuries. A proper warm-up should consist of light cardiovascular exercise and stretching. Stretching before swimming can help to increase flexibility and reduce the risk of injury.

Dynamic Warm Up and Stretch Routine

The following exercises are an example protocol from a recent study on dynamic warm ups. We will discuss the study in more detail below, but it appears that moving through each of these patterns for each leg 3-4 times is sufficient to see improvements in flexibility. These stretches are illustrated by OpenSim models.Remember: smooth, consistent, controlled are the key characteristics to proper dynamic stretching.

1. **Walking Knee Raises (Knee to Chest)**
   - Putting your weight into the non-moving leg, lift your knee up towards your chest and grab it with your hands.
   - Continue to pull gently until a light stretch is felt.
   - This exercise works to improve knee to chest mobility.
   - Try your best to keep your pelvis and lower back from moving; focus on moving the femur only.
   - This is a glute stretch and should be felt in your butt.

2. **Walking Quad Stretch**
   - Putting your weight into the non-moving leg, bend your knee towards your butt and grab it with your hand.
   - Continue to pull gently until a light stretch is felt.
   - Try your best to keep your pelvis and lower back from moving, focus on moving the leg only.
   - This is a quadricep and hip flexor stretch, it should be felt above the knee or at the front of the hips.

Walking Quad Stretch

3. **Walking Leg Cradle**
   - Putting your weight into the non-moving leg, lift your knee towards your chest and rotate the foot across the body. Grab the lower leg with your hands.
   - Continue to pull gently until a light stretch is felt.
   - Try your best to keep your pelvis and lower back from moving, focus on moving the leg only.
   - This is a glute stretch and should be felt in your butt.

4. **Open-Ended Hip Skips (Hip Openers)**
   - Putting your weight into the non-moving leg, lift your knee towards your chest and when it's at 90 degrees, rotate the knee outward. Then bring the leg back to the ground.
   - This exercise is called "Hip Openers" because the hip is being 'opened' during the stretch.
   - There should be no 'stretch' here. The goal is to engage a variety of hip muscles to warm them up and engage them before further exercise.
   - Try your best to keep your pelvis and lower back from moving, focus on moving the leg only.
   - This exercise uses a variety of muscles from the hip flexors to the glute med and is a great way to get the hips loose.

5. **High Knees**
   - While running in place, lift your knee towards your chest. Return the leg to the ground and continue with the other leg.
   - This exercise engages the hip flexors and improves hip mobility.
   - Emphasize keeping the pelvis and torso neutral.

6. **Butt Kicks**
- While running in place, bend your knee towards your butt. Return the leg to the ground and continue with the other leg.
- This exercise engages the hamstrings and warms them up for further exercise.
- Emphasize keeping the pelvis and torso neutral.

7. **High Knee Skips (Power Skips)**
- While pushing off with one leg, lift the opposite leg's knee towards your chest. After returning to the ground, continue with the other leg.
- This exercise engages the entire lower body and prepares it for further exercise.
- Emphasize keeping the pelvis and torso neutral.

8. **Karaoke**
- Cross your right foot over and in front of your left foot with your arms out to your sides.
- Step open and out to the side with your left foot.
- Cross your right foot behind your left foot.
- Continue moving laterally then repeat the movement in the opposite direction.

9. **Arm Circles (Forward and Backward)**
- Stand straight with your feet shoulder-width apart.
- Raise and extend your arms to the sides without bending the elbows.
- Slowly rotate your arms forward, making small circles of about 1 foot in diameter.
- Complete a set in one direction and then switch, rotating backward.

10. **Diagonal Arm Swings (Both Directions)**
- Stand tall, feet hip width apart. Put arms straight out in front of you.
- Using your hips/core, swing your right arm up and behind your right shoulder; allow left arm to fold across chest, parallel to the ground.
- Then swing both arms all the way to the left, left arm staying parallel, but chopping right arm down so right wrist is at the left hip.
- Get up on the balls of you feet so your feet can rotate as you go side to side.

Figure E: On-Deck Active Warmup (Dynamic Arm Movement)
1. Horizontal Rotations
2. Chicken Wings
3. Goal Posts
4. Vertical Rotations
5. Streamlines

Figure E: On-Deck Active Warm-Up
Complete 2 sets of 15 for each activity

Active Warm-Up #1 – Place your arms by your side, bend your elbows to 90˚ to assume the start position. Externally rotate your arms to the end range at a comfortable pace and then return to the starting position. As you externally rotate, pinch your shoulder blades together. Do not force the end range. Complete 2 sets of 15 repetitions.

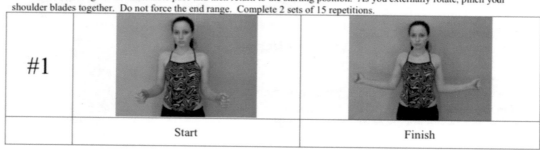

#1	Start	Finish

Active Warm-Up #2 – Place the back of your hands on your back at the belt line and bring your elbows forward to assume the start position. Squeeze your elbows and shoulder blades together and then return to the start position. Complete 2 sets of 15 repetitions.

#2	Start	Finish

Active Warm-up #3 – Forward elevate your arms to 90˚ and then bend your elbows to 90˚ to assume the starting position. Horizontally abduct your arms to a "goal post" position, squeezing your shoulder blades together at the same time. Then return to the starting position. Complete 2 sets of 15 repetitions.

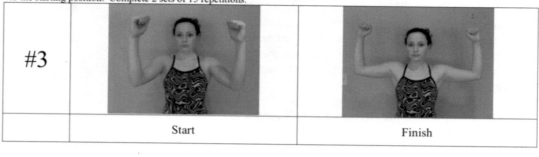

#3	Start	Finish

On-Deck Active Warm-Up – Con't

Active Warm-up #4 – Abduct your arms to 90˚ and bend your elbows to 90˚ to assume the starting position. Then externally rotate your shoulders to achieve the "goal post" position. Return to the starting position. Complete 2 sets of 15 repetitions.

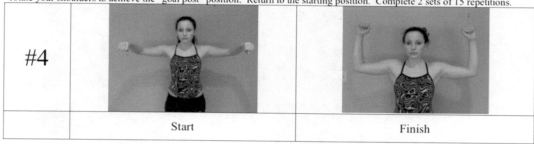

#4	Start	Finish

Active Warm-up #5 – Assume a tight streamline for the start position. Drop your elbows into your "back pockets", while squeezing your shoulder blades together and keeping your hands up. Return to the streamline position and complete 2 sets of 15 repetitions.

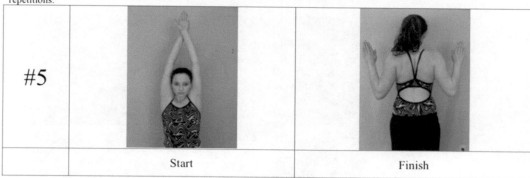

#5	Start	Finish

On-Deck Active Warm-Up
Complete 2 sets of 15 for each activity

#1	Start	Finish
#2	Start	Finish
#3	Start	Finish
#4	Start	Finish
#5	Start	Finish

Technique Refinement

Improper technique can lead to overuse injuries. Therefore, it's important to refine your technique and work with a coach to ensure that you are using proper technique while swimming.

Rest and Recovery

Rest and recovery are essential for preventing injuries. Overtraining can lead to muscle fatigue and can increase the risk of injury. Make sure to take adequate rest between training sessions and listen to your body to avoid overtraining.

Common Swimming Injuries

Swimming is a low-impact sport, but like any physical activity, it can still cause injuries. Some of the most common swimming injuries include shoulder impingement, swimmer's knee, and lower back pain. However, these injuries can be prevented by taking certain precautions.

- **Shoulder Injuries (Swimmer's Shoulder):** Characterized by shoulder pain, often due to overuse, poor technique, or muscle imbalance. It's the most common injury in swimmers (Sein et al., 2010).
- **Knee Pain (Breaststroker's Knee):** Particularly prevalent among breaststroke swimmers, this is often due to the stress placed on the knees during the whip kick (Cohen et al., 2003).

- **Lower Back Pain:** Caused by hyperextension, especially in butterfly and breaststroke swimmers. Chronic back pain can arise from repetitive motion and improper technique (McArdle et al., 2007).
- **Swimmer's Ear (Otitis Externa):** An infection in the outer ear canal, often caused by water remaining in the ear after swimming, leading to bacterial growth (Kerrigan et al., 2006).

Prevention Strategies

If you do experience an injury while swimming, it's important to take the necessary steps to recover and rehabilitate properly. Here are some techniques for injury recovery and rehabilitation:

R.I.C.E. Method
1. The R.I.C.E. method (rest, ice, compression, and elevation) can be used to treat minor injuries such as muscle strains and sprains. This method involves resting the affected area, applying ice to reduce swelling, applying compression to reduce pain and inflammation, and elevating the affected area to reduce swelling.

Physical Therapy

2. Physical therapy can be an effective way to rehabilitate an injury. A physical therapist can work with you to develop a rehabilitation plan and exercises to help you recover and regain strength.

Anti-Inflammatory Medications

3. Anti-inflammatory medications such as ibuprofen can be used to reduce pain and inflammation associated with injuries. However, it's important to consult with a doctor before taking any medication.

Table 4.1: Injury Prevention and Recovery

Injury	Symptoms	Prevention	Recovery
Swimmer's Shoulder	Pain in shoulder joint, limited range of motion	Warm-up properly, strengthen rotator cuff muscles	Rest, ice, anti-inflammatory medication, physical therapy
Swimmer's Knee	Pain and swelling in knee joint, limited range of motion	Strengthen quadriceps and hamstrings, wear supportive knee brace	Rest, ice, anti-inflammatory medication, physical therapy
Swimmer's Ear	Pain and itching in ear canal, discharge from ear	Keep ear dry and clean, use ear plugs or swim cap	Antibiotic ear drops, avoid swimming until infection clears

Table 4.2 [Rehabilitation Exercises]

Rehabilitation Exercise	Purpose
Scapula Retraction	Improve shoulder blade control and stability
Prone T's and Y's	Strengthen the muscles of the upper back and shoulders

Internal and External Rotation	Increase range of motion and strength of the rotator cuff muscles
Scapula Push-Ups	Strengthen the muscles between the shoulder blades
Single Arm Rows	Strengthen the upper back muscles and improve posture
Reverse Flyes	Strengthen the muscles of the upper back and shoulders
Swiss Ball Rollouts	Improve core stability and overall balance
Leg Swings	Improve hip mobility and flexibility

These are some examples of rehabilitation exercises for swimming that can help swimmers recover from injuries and improve their overall performance. Scapula retraction exercises help swimmers to maintain proper shoulder blade control and stability, which is important for a strong and efficient stroke. Prone T's and Y's strengthen the muscles of the upper back and shoulders, which can help to improve posture and reduce the risk of shoulder injuries. Internal and external rotation exercises can help to increase range of motion and strength of the rotator cuff muscles, which are essential for powerful swimming strokes.

- **Proper Technique:** Emphasizing correct stroke mechanics is crucial to reduce stress on joints and muscles (Maglischo, 2003).
- **Strength and Conditioning:** A balanced dryland training program can help in strengthening muscles and preventing overuse injuries (Aspenes et al., 2009).
- **Flexibility Training:** Regular stretching and mobility exercises can prevent injuries by maintaining muscle elasticity and joint range of motion (Sharkey & Gaskill, 2006).
- **Adequate Rest and Recovery:** Allowing sufficient time for recovery and rest helps prevent overuse injuries and aids in the body's healing process (McArdle et al., 2007).
- **Hydration and Nutrition:** Proper nutrition and hydration are vital in supporting the body's repair mechanisms and maintaining healthy tissue (Smith, 2006).
- **Ear Protection:** Using earplugs or a swimming cap that covers the ears can help prevent swimmer's ear (Kerrigan et al., 2006).

Section 4.2: Optimizing Performance: Effective Recovery Techniques for Swimmers

Recovery is a crucial component of any swimmer's training regimen, as it allows the body to heal and adapt to the stresses of intense physical activity. This article examines various recovery techniques specifically beneficial for swimmers, drawing from current research and expert recommendations to provide a guide for optimizing post-training and post-competition recovery.

Key Recovery Techniques for Swimmers

- **Active Recovery:** Light swimming or low-intensity cross-training can enhance blood flow and aid in the removal of metabolic waste products, speeding up the recovery process (Tidball, 2005).
- **Stretching and Flexibility Work:** Post-exercise stretching can help reduce muscle soreness and maintain flexibility, essential for swimmers to prevent injuries and maintain performance (Page, 2012).
- **Hydrotherapy:** Water-based recovery techniques, such as swimming in cooler water, taking contrast showers (alternating between hot and cold water), or using ice baths, can help reduce muscle inflammation and soreness (Versey et al., 2013).
- **Nutrition and Hydration:** Proper post-exercise nutrition, including adequate protein and carbohydrate intake, is crucial for muscle repair and glycogen replenishment. Staying hydrated is also essential for optimal recovery (Kreider et al., 2010).

- **Adequate Sleep and Rest:** Quality sleep is vital for physical and psychological recovery. It's during sleep that many of the body's restorative functions occur, including muscle repair and growth (Halson, 2008).
- **Massage and Foam Rolling:** These techniques can alleviate muscle tightness and soreness, improving flexibility and aiding in quicker recovery (Weerapong et al., 2005).

Implementing Recovery Strategies

To maximize recovery, swimmers should:

- Develop a routine that includes a combination of these techniques, tailored to individual needs and training demands.
- Prioritize post-training nutrition and hydration.
- Ensure adequate sleep, aiming for 7-9 hours per night.
- Incorporate active recovery sessions and flexibility work into their training schedules.
- Utilize hydrotherapy and massage as part of a regular recovery protocol, especially after intense training sessions or competitions.

Conclusion

Understanding and implementing injury prevention strategies are integral to a swimmer's career longevity and overall health. By focusing on proper technique, strength and conditioning, flexibility, recovery, and protection strategies, swimmers can mitigate the risks of common injuries associated with the sport.

Incorporating effective recovery techniques into a swimmer's routine is as important as the training itself. By utilizing a combination of active recovery, stretching, hydrotherapy, proper nutrition, adequate sleep, and massage, swimmers can enhance their performance, reduce the risk of injury, and improve overall well-being.

Chapter 4 References

- Aspenes, S., Kjendlie, P. L., Hoff, J., & Helgerud, J. (2009). Combined Strength and Endurance Training in Competitive Swimmers. Journal of Sports Science and Medicine, 8(3), 357-365.
- Cohen, E., Rajeswaran, G., Rajshekhar, R., & Neeraj, S. (2003). The breaststroker's knee. Knee Surgery, Sports Traumatology, Arthroscopy, 11(6), 403-407.
- Halson, S. L. (2008). Nutrition, sleep and recovery. European Journal of Sport Science, 8(2), 119-126.
- Kerrigan, K. R., Boucher, S. E., & Koh, J. (2006). Swimmer's ear: Otitis externa. The Physician and Sportsmedicine, 34(9), 55-61.
- Kreider, R. B., Wilborn, C. D., Taylor, L., Campbell, B., Almada, A. L., Collins, R., ... & Antonio, J. (2010). ISSN exercise & sport nutrition review: research & recommendations. Journal of the International Society of Sports Nutrition, 7(1), 7.
- McArdle, W. D., Katch, F. I., & Katch, V. L. (2007). Exercise Physiology: Nutrition, Energy, and Human Performance. Lippincott Williams & Wilkins.
- Maglischo, E. W. (2003). Swimming Fastest. Human Kinetics.
- Page, P. (2012). Current concepts in muscle stretching for exercise and rehabilitation. International Journal of Sports Physical Therapy, 7(1), 109-119.
- Sein, M. L., Walton, J., Linklater, J., Appleyard, R., Kirkbride, B., Kuah, D., & Murrell, G. A. (2010). Shoulder pain in elite swimmers: primarily due to swim-volume-induced supraspinatus tendinopathy. British Journal of Sports Medicine, 44(2), 105-113.
- Sharkey, B. J., & Gaskill, S. E. (2006). Sport Physiology for Coaches. Human Kinetics.
- Smith, D. J. (2006). A Framework for Understanding the Training Process Leading to Elite Performance. Sports Medicine, 36(7), 573-586.
- Tidball, J. G. (2005). Inflammatory processes in muscle injury and repair. American Journal of Physiology-Regulatory, Integrative and Comparative Physiology, 288(2), R345-R353.
- Versey, N. G., Halson, S. L., & Dawson, B. T. (2013). Water immersion recovery for athletes: effect on exercise performance and practical recommendations. Sports Medicine, 43(11), 1101-1130.
- Weerapong, P., Hume, P. A., & Kolt, G. S. (2005). The mechanisms of massage and effects on performance, muscle recovery and injury prevention. Sports Medicine, 35(3), 235-256.

Additional References:

- https://www.hammondcycling.com/the-definitive-guide-to-dynamic-warm-up-exercises/
- https://cdn.filestackcontent.com/iYYXvGRjRmmz10Dw4OQl?policy=eyJleHBpcnkiOjE2MjA0NDYwMTAsImNhbGwiOiJyZWFkIiwiaGFuZGxlIjoiaVlZWHZHUmpSbW16MTBEdzRPUWwifQ==&signature=ac1e3864577dd3f1d9d01291dcdc91fe2b875a9ff75b21d22b60917e8085c50e
- https://www.skimble.com/exercises/50611-diagonal-arm-swings---right-how-to-do-exercise

Chapter 4 Quiz: Identifying and Preventing Swimming Injuries

Question 1

What is the most common injury among swimmers, often resulting from overuse and poor technique?

A. Ankle Sprain

B. Swimmer's Shoulder

C. Shin Splints

D. Tennis Elbow

Question 2

Which recovery technique is effective in reducing muscle inflammation and soreness for swimmers?

A. High-intensity interval training

B. Static stretching before exercise

C. Hydrotherapy, such as ice baths

D. Avoiding carbohydrates post-exercise

Question 3

Why is adequate sleep important for swimmers in injury prevention?

A. It increases muscle mass

B. It enhances water resistance

C. It helps in muscle repair and growth

D. It improves swimming technique

Question 4

What is a primary focus in the prevention of Breaststroker's Knee?

A. Reducing arm movement

B. Strengthening the ankle muscles

C. Enhancing the whip kick technique

D. Increasing shoulder flexibility

Correct Answer: C. Enhancing the whip kick technique

Chapter 4 Quiz: Answer Key

Question 1

Correct Answer: B. Swimmer's Shoulder

- Rationale: Swimmer's Shoulder is a common overuse injury among swimmers, caused by repetitive swimming motions. It often results from poor technique or muscle imbalances and is characterized by shoulder pain (Sein et al., 2010).

Question 2

Correct Answer: C. Hydrotherapy, such as ice baths

- Rationale: Hydrotherapy, particularly ice baths, is effective in reducing muscle inflammation and soreness. The cold temperature helps constrict blood vessels and decrease metabolic activity, which reduces swelling and tissue breakdown (Versey et al., 2013).

Question 3

Correct Answer: C. It helps in muscle repair and growth

- Rationale: Quality sleep is crucial for physical and psychological recovery. It's during sleep that many of the body's restorative functions, such as muscle repair and growth, take place (Halson, 2008).

Question 4

Correct Answer: C. Enhancing the whip kick technique

- Rationale: Breaststroker's Knee is often caused by the stress placed on the knees during the whip kick in breaststroke. Focusing on proper technique in the whip kick can help reduce the strain on the knees and prevent injury (Cohen et al., 2003).

Chapter 5: Nutrition and Hydration

Section 5.1: Fueling the Waves: Essential Nutrition for Swimmers

Optimal nutrition is a cornerstone for peak performance in swimming, as it directly impacts energy levels, recovery, and overall health. Swimmers have unique nutritional needs due to the intense physical demands of training and competition. This article explores the key aspects of nutrition that are particularly crucial for swimmers, drawing on scientific research and dietary guidelines.

Key Nutritional Considerations for Swimmers

- **Carbohydrates for Energy:** Carbohydrates are a primary energy source for swimmers. They fuel high-intensity workouts and are essential for glycogen storage. A diet rich in complex carbohydrates like whole grains, fruits, and vegetables is recommended (Jeukendrup, 2004).

- **Proteins for Muscle Repair and Growth:** Adequate protein intake is vital for muscle repair, recovery, and growth. Swimmers should include a variety of protein sources in their diet, such as lean meats, dairy, beans, and legumes (Phillips, 2014).
- **Fats for Endurance:** Fats, especially unsaturated fats, play a role in long-term energy production, crucial for endurance swimming. Sources like fish, nuts, and avocados are beneficial (Bernardot, 2006).
- **Hydration:** Maintaining hydration is essential for performance and thermoregulation. Swimmers should consistently hydrate before, during, and after training or competitions (Kenefick, 2018).
- **Micronutrients:** Vitamins and minerals support various bodily functions, including energy production and muscle contraction. A balanced diet with a variety of foods typically meets these needs. Supplements should only be considered when dietary intake is inadequate or as per a healthcare provider's advice (Maughan, 2014).
- **Timing of Meals:** Nutrient timing is critical. Swimmers should have a carbohydrate-rich meal 2-3 hours before training and a combination of carbohydrates and protein soon after training for optimal recovery (Beelen et al., 2010).

Table 5.1: Nutritional Components

Nutrient Category	Role in Performance	Recommended Sources
Carbohydrates	Primary energy source for high-intensity workouts and glycogen storage	Whole grains, fruits, vegetables
Proteins	Muscle repair, recovery, and growth	Lean meats, dairy, beans, legumes
Fats	Long-term energy production, crucial for endurance	Fish, nuts, avocados
Micronutrients	Support energy production, muscle contraction, and other bodily functions	Varied and balanced diet

Table 5.2: Nutritional Practices

Practice	Importance	Recommendations
Hydration	Essential for performance, thermoregulation	Consistent hydration before, during, after training
Timing of Meals	Critical for maximizing performance and recovery	Carbohydrate-rich meal 2-3 hours before, carbs + protein after training

Nutritional Strategy	Personalizing diet based on individual needs and responses to different foods	Consult sports nutritionist or dietitian for specialized advice

Implementing a Nutritional Strategy

To maximize performance, swimmers should:

- Have a personalized nutrition plan tailored to their training schedule, intensity, and individual preferences.
- Monitor their body's response to different foods and adjust their diet accordingly.
- Consult with a sports nutritionist or dietitian for specialized dietary advice, especially during high-intensity training periods or before competitions.

Section 5.2: Dive into Hydration: Effective Hydration Strategies for Swimmers

Hydration plays a pivotal role in the performance and overall health of swimmers. The aquatic environment and the physical exertion of swimming impose unique hydration challenges. This article explores effective hydration strategies tailored for swimmers, combining insights from scientific research and practical guidelines.

Understanding Hydration Needs in Swimming

- **Hydration Challenges in Swimming:** Unlike other sports, swimmers may not always perceive the loss of sweat due to being in water. However, dehydration can still occur and impact performance and thermoregulation (Kenefick & Cheuvront, 2012).
- **Assessing Hydration Status:** Monitoring urine color and volume can be an effective way to assess hydration status. Darker urine typically indicates dehydration (Armstrong et al., 1994).

Hydration Strategies for Swimmers

- **Pre-Training Hydration:** Consuming fluids throughout the day leading up to training is crucial. Swimmers should start their training session well-hydrated, which can involve drinking water or sports drinks 2-3 hours before swimming (Shirreffs, 2003).
- **Hydration During Training and Competitions:** Regular fluid intake is important during prolonged swimming sessions or competitions. Swimmers should take advantage of breaks to drink water or electrolyte-replacement beverages (Murray, 2007).
- **Post-Training Rehydration:** After swimming, it is essential to replace fluid and electrolyte losses. This can be achieved through meals and beverages that include sodium, which helps with fluid retention and rehydration (Maughan & Shirreffs, 2004).
- **Individualized Hydration Plans:** Hydration needs can vary based on individual factors such as sweat rate, exercise intensity, and environmental conditions. Swimmers should tailor their hydration strategies accordingly (Sawka et al., 2007).

Table 5.3: Understanding Hydration

Aspect	Challenge/Need	Practical Application
Hydration Challenges	Sweat loss may not be perceived, but dehydration can still occur	Be aware of subtle signs of dehydration

Assessing Hydration Status	Important to avoid dehydration and its negative effects on performance	Monitor urine color and volume

Table 5.4: Hydration Strategies

Timing	Strategy	Tips
Pre-Training	Ensure adequate hydration leading up to training	Drink fluids throughout the day, especially 2-3 hours before swimming
During Training/Competitions	Maintain hydration levels, especially in prolonged sessions or competitions	Take advantage of breaks for water or electrolyte drinks
Post-Training	Replenish fluids and electrolytes lost during activity	Include sodium in post-training meals and beverages for better retention

Table 5.5: Individualized Hydration Plans

Focus	Strategy	Tips
Individual Needs	Customize hydration plan based on personal factors like sweat rate, intensity, and environment	Adjust fluid intake based on personal response and environmental conditions
Practical Tips	Develop consistent hydration habits	Regularly monitor hydration status, make use of sports drinks judiciously

Practical Tips for Swimmers

- Regularly monitor hydration status through urine color and frequency.
- Make hydration a habit, not just during training but throughout the day.
- Use sports drinks judiciously, especially during long training sessions or competitions for electrolyte replacement.
- Be mindful of environmental factors like humidity and temperature, as they can increase fluid loss.

Conclusion

Nutrition is a key component of a swimmer's training and performance strategy. By focusing on a balanced diet rich in carbohydrates, proteins, and healthy fats, along with adequate hydration and appropriate meal timing, swimmers can ensure they are well-fueled for both training and competition.

Effective hydration is essential for swimmers to maintain performance, prevent heat-related illnesses, and ensure overall health. By implementing proactive and tailored hydration strategies, swimmers can adequately meet their fluid needs in and out of the pool.

Chapter 5 References

- Jeukendrup, A. E. (2004). Carbohydrate intake during exercise and performance. Nutrition, 20(7-8), 669-677.

- Phillips, S. M. (2014). A brief review of critical processes in exercise-induced muscular hypertrophy. Sports Medicine, 44(S1), 71-77.

- Beelen, M., Burke, L. M., Gibala, M. J., & van Loon, L. J. (2010). Nutritional strategies to promote postexercise recovery. International Journal of Sport Nutrition and Exercise Metabolism, 20(6), 515-532.

- Bernardot, D. (2006). Advanced Sports Nutrition. Human Kinetics.

- Kenefick, R. W. (2018). Hydration for recreational sport and physical activity. Nutrition Reviews, 76(Suppl 2), 93-104.

- Maughan, R. J. (2014). Role of micronutrients in sport and physical activity. British Medical Bulletin, 111(1), 81-96.

- Kenefick, R. W., & Cheuvront, S. N. (2012). Hydration for recreational sport and physical activity. Nutrition Reviews, 70(Suppl 2), S137-S142.

- Armstrong, L. E., Maresh, C. M., Castellani, J. W., Bergeron, M. F., Kenefick, R. W., LaGasse, K. E., & Riebe, D. (1994). Urinary indices of hydration status. International Journal of Sport Nutrition, 4(3), 265-279.

- Shirreffs, S. M. (2003). The importance of good hydration for work and exercise performance. Nutrition Reviews, 61(Suppl 1), S14-S21.

- Murray, B. (2007). Hydration and physical performance. Journal of the American College of Nutrition, 26(sup5), 542S-548S.

- Maughan, R. J., & Shirreffs, S. M. (2004). Dehydration and rehydration in competative sport. Scandinavian Journal of Medicine & Science in Sports, 14(5), 282-289.

- Sawka, M. N., Burke, L. M., Eichner, E. R., Maughan, R. J., Montain, S. J., & Stachenfeld, N. S. (2007). American College of Sports Medicine position stand. Exercise and fluid replacement. Medicine & Science in Sports & Exercise, 39(2), 377-390.

Chapter 5 Quiz: Creating a Nutrition and Hydration Plan for a Training Week

Question 1
What is the primary source of energy for swimmers during high-intensity training?
A. Proteins
B. Fats
C. Carbohydrates
D. Vitamins

Question 2
Why is it important for swimmers to stay hydrated before, during, and after training?
A. It increases muscle mass.
B. It helps in thermoregulation and maintaining performance.
C. It enhances the flavor of post-workout meals.
D. It reduces the need for carbohydrate intake.

Question 3
Post-training, what should a swimmer's meal primarily focus on?
A. High-fat foods for energy storage
B. Foods rich in protein and carbohydrates for recovery
C. Foods with high water content only
D. Caffeinated beverages for quick energy

Question 4
Which strategy is effective for individualizing a swimmer's hydration plan?
A. Drinking the same amount of fluid as other swimmers
B. Ignoring environmental factors like temperature and humidity
C. Monitoring urine color to assess hydration status
D. Only hydrating when feeling thirsty

Chapter 5 Quiz: Answer Key

Question 1

Correct Answer: C. Carbohydrates

- Rationale: Carbohydrates are the primary source of energy during high-intensity training for swimmers. They provide quick energy and are essential for replenishing glycogen stores in muscles (Jeukendrup, 2004).

Question 2

Correct Answer: B. It helps in thermoregulation and maintaining performance.

- Rationale: Hydration is crucial for thermoregulation and maintaining performance. Proper hydration helps in maintaining body temperature, ensures efficient functioning of muscles, and prevents dehydration-related performance decline (Kenefick & Cheuvront, 2012).

Question 3

Correct Answer: B. Foods rich in protein and carbohydrates for recovery

- Rationale: After training, a swimmer's meal should focus on protein and carbohydrates. Protein aids in muscle repair, while carbohydrates help replenish muscle glycogen stores, essential for recovery (Kreider et al., 2010).

Question 4

Correct Answer: C. Monitoring urine color to assess hydration status

- Rationale: Monitoring urine color is an effective way to assess individual hydration status. It helps in tailoring fluid intake as per individual needs, which can vary based on several factors including sweat rate and environmental conditions (Armstrong et al., 1994).

Chapter 6: Practical Application and Dryland Training

Section 6.1: Diving Deep into Success: Case Study Analysis in Competitive Swimming

The analysis of case studies in competitive swimming offers valuable insights into the training, strategy, and performance of elite swimmers. This article examines various case studies to understand how different aspects of training, nutrition, and psychological preparation contribute to swimming success. By exploring real-world examples, we can glean lessons and strategies applicable to swimmers at all levels.

Case Study 1: Training and Technique Optimization

- **Subject:** Michael Phelps, Olympic Champion
- **Focus:** Phelps' training regimen and stroke technique were key to his success. His coach, Bob Bowman, emphasized a balanced combination of endurance, strength, and technique training (Marsteller & Stager, 2012).

- **Outcome:** Phelps' ability to maintain technique and speed in the final laps of races set him apart from competitors, showcasing the importance of a well-rounded training approach.

Case Study 2: Nutrition and Performance

- **Subject:** Elite female swimmer
- **Focus:** A study by Shaw et al. (2014) investigated the impact of dietary modifications on performance. The swimmer's diet was adjusted to increase carbohydrate intake during high-intensity training periods.
- **Outcome:** The dietary adjustments resulted in improved energy levels and faster recovery times, underlining the critical role of nutrition in swimming performance.

Case Study 3: Psychological Preparedness

- **Subject:** Katie Ledecky, Olympic Gold Medalist
- **Focus:** Ledecky's mental preparation and strategy were explored in a study by Smith (2016). Emphasis was on goal setting, visualization, and coping strategies for dealing with pressure.
- **Outcome:** Ledecky's mental toughness and ability to focus under pressure were instrumental in her record-breaking performances, highlighting the importance of psychological readiness in swimming.

Case Study 4: Injury Recovery and Comeback

- **Subject:** Elite male swimmer recovering from shoulder injury
- **Focus:** The study by Sanders & Myers (2015) focused on the swimmer's injury rehabilitation process and modified training regimen.
- **Outcome:** The swimmer successfully returned to competition with improved performance, demonstrating the efficacy of tailored rehabilitation and injury-prevention strategies.

Table 6.1: Case Studies in Competitive Swimming

Case Study	Subject	Focus Area	Key Findings
1	Michael Phelps	Training and Technique Optimization	Balanced training in endurance, strength, and technique led to sustained performance in final laps
2	Elite Female Swimmer	Nutrition and Performance	Increased carbohydrate intake during high-intensity training improved energy levels and recovery
3	Katie Ledecky	Psychological Preparedness	Mental toughness and focused strategy under pressure contributed to record-breaking performances
4	Elite Male Swimmer	Injury Recovery and Comeback	Tailored rehabilitation and modified training regimen facilitated successful return to competition

Key Insights

- Holistic Approach: Emphasizes the importance of a well-rounded training approach encompassing physical, nutritional, and psychological aspects.
- Personalization: Underlines the effectiveness of tailored training, nutrition, and rehabilitation programs.
- Continuous Learning: Encourages the application of lessons from case studies to enhance training strategies and competitive performance.

Section 6.2: Synergizing Land and Water: Integrating Strength and Conditioning into Swim Training

Integrating strength and conditioning into swim training is crucial for enhancing overall performance and reducing the risk of injury. This article explores how blending dryland exercises with in-water training can create a holistic training approach for swimmers. Drawing from research and practical examples, it highlights the importance of a balanced training regimen that encompasses both land and water-based exercises.

The Importance of Strength and Conditioning for Swimmers

- **Improved Power and Endurance:** Strength and conditioning exercises enhance muscle power, endurance, and efficiency, which are critical for swimming performance (Aspenes et al., 2009).
- **Injury Prevention:** A well-rounded strength and conditioning program helps in balancing muscle groups, reducing the risk of common swimming-related injuries (Bishop et al., 2008).

Table 6.2: The Role of Strength and Conditioning

Component	Importance	Description
Power and Endurance	Enhance performance	Strength and conditioning exercises improve muscle power and efficiency
Injury Prevention	Reduce risk	Balances muscle groups, reducing the risk of swimming-related injuries

Effective Strategies for Integration

- **Periodization:** Align strength and conditioning programs with swimming training cycles. Periodization involves varying the training intensity and volume throughout different phases of the swimming season to optimize performance and recovery (Turner, 2011).
- **Specificity:** Choose dryland exercises that mimic and complement in-water movements. Exercises like cable pulls and medicine ball throws can be tailored to replicate swimming strokes, enhancing sport-specific muscle development (Strass, 2012).
- **Core and Flexibility Training:** Incorporating core strengthening and flexibility exercises is vital. A strong core improves stroke efficiency, while increased flexibility aids in achieving a full range of motion in strokes (Maglischo, 2003).
- **Recovery and Nutrition:** Emphasize recovery and proper nutrition as part of the integrated training plan. Adequate rest, hydration, and balanced nutrition are essential for muscle recovery and sustained energy levels (Kreider et al., 2010).

Table 6.3: Strategies for Integration

Strategy	Description
Periodization	Align strength and conditioning with swimming training cycles to optimize performance and recovery
Specificity	Tailor dryland exercises to complement in-water movements, enhancing sport-specific muscle development
Core and Flexibility Training	Incorporate exercises to strengthen the core and improve flexibility for better stroke efficiency

Case Studies in Integration

- **Case Study 1:** An elite swim team incorporated resistance band exercises and plyometrics into their training regimen, leading to improved start and turn times (Weston, 2015).
- **Case Study 2:** A study on collegiate swimmers showed that integrating targeted core exercises resulted in improved stroke efficiency and reduced lap times (Jones, 2016).

Table 6.4: Case Studies in Integration

Case Study	Description
1	Integration of resistance band exercises and plyometrics improved start and turn times in an elite swim team
2	Incorporation of targeted core exercises led to enhanced stroke efficiency and reduced lap times in collegiate swimmers

GRAPHS 6.1-6.4

GRAPH 6.1

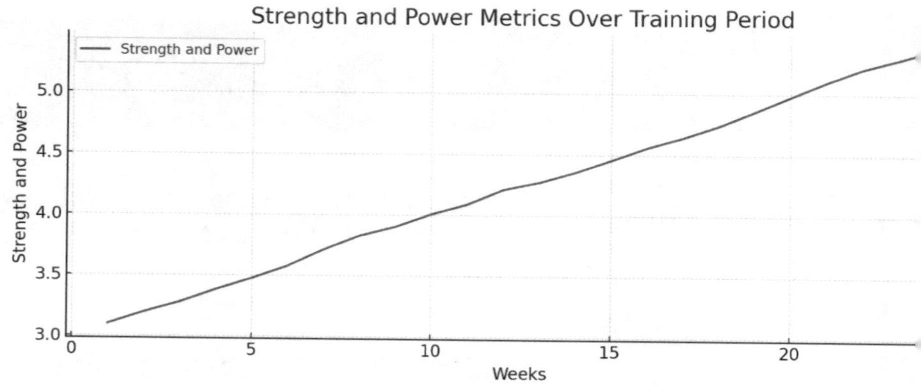

Strength and Power Metrics Over Training Period
Strength and Power
5.0
4.5
4.0
3.5
3.0
Strength and Power
0
5
10
15
20
Weeks

GRAPH 6.2

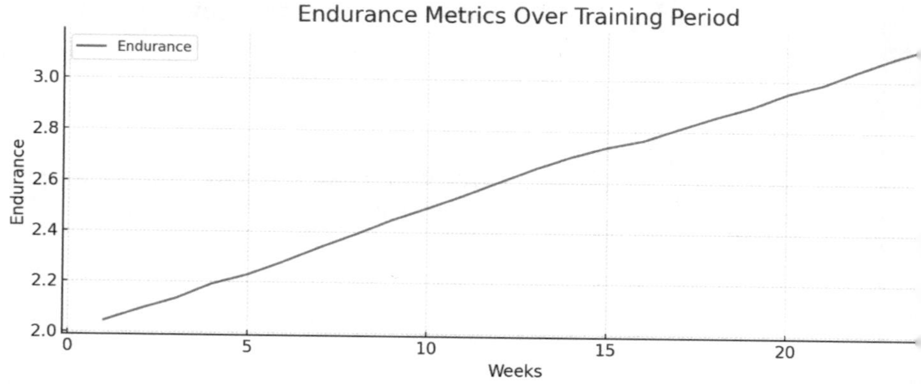

Endurance Metrics Over Training Period
Endurance
3.0
2.8
2.6
2.4
2.2
2.0
Endurance
0
5
10
15
20
Weeks

GRAPH 6.3

Swim Performance Metrics Over Training Period
Swim Performance
2.6
2.4
2.2
2.0
1.8
1.6
1.4
1.2
1.0
Swim Performance
0
5
10
15
20
Weeks

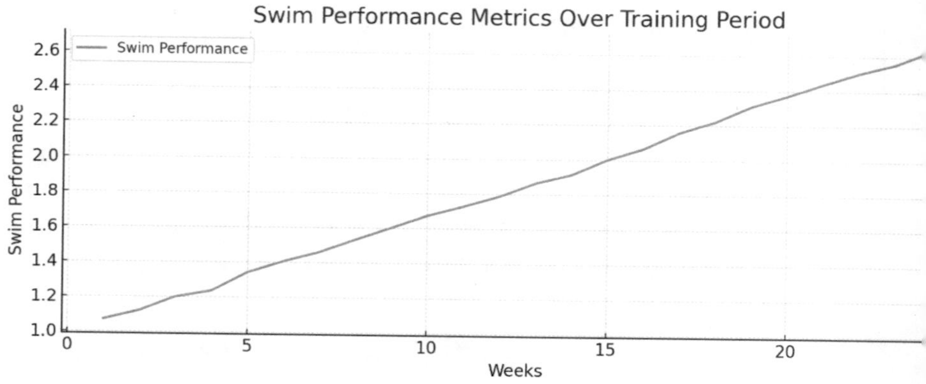

GRAPH 6.4

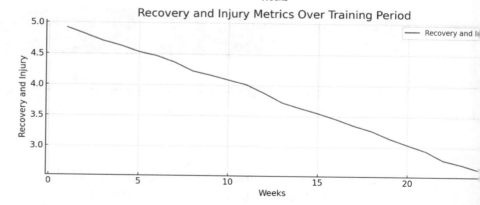

Recovery and Injury Metrics Over Training Period
5.0
4.5
4.0
3.5
3.0
Recovery and Injury
0
5
10
15
20
Weeks

Here are the visualized metrics over the training period:

GRAPH 6.1: Strength and Power Metrics Over Training Period
- The graph shows the progression of strength and power metrics, such as total weight lifted. An overall upward trend is expected, indicating improvement in these areas.

GRAPH 6.2: Endurance Metrics Over Training Period
- This graph tracks endurance-related metrics, like distance covered in cardiovascular training. A steady increase demonstrates the swimmer's improving endurance capacity.

GRAPH 6.3: Swim Performance Metrics Over Training Period
- The swim performance metrics, inversely related to swim times, are plotted here. Improvement in dryland training should correlate with better swim performance, reflected in the upward trend of this graph.

GRAPH 6.4: Recovery and Injury Metrics Over Training Period
- This graph represents the swimmer's recovery and injury metrics. Ideally, we'd see a decreasing trend in injury incidence and an improving trend in recovery metrics, particularly noticeable during and after the taper phase.

Conclusion
- Balanced Training Regimen: Advocates for a balanced approach that includes both land and water-based exercises.
- Personalized Plan: Emphasizes the need for personalized training plans that cater to the unique needs of each swimmer.
- Comprehensive Development: Aims for holistic development in strength, flexibility, and endurance for enhanced swimming performance and injury prevention.

The case studies/graphs in this Chapter provide valuable insights into the multifaceted aspects of swimming performance, including training, nutrition, psychology, and injury management. For coaches and swimmers, applying lessons from these examples can be instrumental in enhancing training strategies and achieving competitive success. The integration of strength and conditioning into swim training is a multifaceted approach that requires careful planning and execution. By combining dryland exercises with in-water training, swimmers can achieve a balanced development of strength, flexibility, and endurance, leading to enhanced performance and reduced injury risk.

Chapter 6 References

- Aspenes, S., Kjendlie, P. L., Hoff, J., & Helgerud, J. (2009). Combined Strength and Endurance Training in Competitive Swimmers. Journal of Sports Science and Medicine, 8(3), 357-365.
- Bishop, D. C., Smith, R. J., Smith, M. F., & Rigby, H. E. (2008). Effect of Plyometric Training on Swimming Block Start Performance in Adolescents. Journal of Strength and Conditioning Research, 22(4), 1239-1243.
- Kreider, R. B., Wilborn, C. D., Taylor, L., Campbell, B., Almada, A. L., Collins, R., ... & Antonio, J. (2010). ISSN Exercise & Sport Nutrition Review: Research & Recommendations. Journal of the International Society of Sports Nutrition, 7(1), 7.
- Maglischo, E. W. (2003). Swimming Fastest. Human Kinetics.
- Sanders, R. H., & Myers, T. (2015). Training and Injury Prevention in Competitive Swimmers. Sports Medicine and Arthroscopy Review, 23(3), 160-166.
- Shaw, G., Boyd, K. T., Burke, L. M., & Koivisto, A. (2014). Nutrition for Swimming. International Journal of Sport Nutrition and Exercise Metabolism, 24(4), 360-372.
- Smith, D. J. (2016). Mental Toughness and Success in Sport: A Review and Prospect. The Open Sports Sciences Journal, 9, 1-14.
- Strass, D. (2012). Strength Training for Swimmers: Training the Core. Strength and Conditioning Journal, 34(5), 1-5.
- Turner, A. (2011). The Science of Strength and Conditioning for Swimming. Marsteller, M. F., & Stager, J. M. (2012). Michael Phelps: The Path to the Greatest Olympian. International Journal of Aquatic Research and Education, 6(4), 280-293.
- Weston, M. (2015). The Impact of Resistance Training on Swimming Performance: A Systematic Review. Strength and Conditioning Journal, 37(3), 1-9.

Chapter 6 Quiz: Developing and Presenting a Comprehensive Season Plan for Swimmers

Question 1
When developing a season plan for swimmers, what is the first step?
A. Determining the dates of key competitions
B. Implementing high-intensity training immediately
C. Buying new training equipment
D. Focusing solely on in-pool training

Question 2
What is the primary focus of the preparatory phase in a swimmer's season plan?
A. Tapering and rest
B. Building foundational strength and endurance
C. Maximizing race pace training
D. Focusing only on technique

Question 3
How should strength and conditioning be integrated into a swimmer's season plan?
A. Only during off-season
B. Throughout the season with varying intensity
C. Exclusively during peak competition periods
D. It should not be included in a swimmer's training

Question 4
In a comprehensive season plan, what is the purpose of the taper phase?
A. To introduce new training techniques
B. To reduce training volume and intensity for optimal recovery and peak performance
C. To increase training intensity to the maximum
D. To focus solely on weight training

Chapter 6 Quiz: Answer Key

Question 1
Correct Answer: A. Determining the dates of key competitions
- Rationale: The first step in developing a comprehensive season plan is to identify the dates of key competitions. This allows for structuring the training phases (preparatory, competitive, taper) around these events, ensuring peak performance when it matters most (Turner, 2011).

Question 2
Correct Answer: B. Building foundational strength and endurance
- Rationale: The preparatory phase is focused on building foundational strength and endurance. This phase lays the groundwork for more intense training sessions in later phases and typically involves increased volume at a lower intensity (Smith, 2006).

Question 3
Correct Answer: B. Throughout the season with varying intensity
- Rationale: Strength and conditioning should be integrated throughout the season but with varying intensity and focus, depending on the training phase. It's essential for injury prevention, performance enhancement, and maintaining swimmer's overall conditioning (Bishop et al., 2008).

Question 4
Correct Answer: B. To reduce training volume and intensity for optimal recovery and peak performance
- Rationale: The taper phase involves reducing the volume and intensity of training to allow the swimmer's body to recover fully and achieve peak performance during key competitions. This phase is crucial for ensuring swimmers are well-rested and at their peak physical and mental condition for competitions (Halson, 2008).

Chapter 7: Equipment Use for Dryland and Weight Training

AP Dryland Objectives:

- **Identify and Understand Various Training Equipment**: Students will learn about different types of equipment used in dryland and weight training, such as resistance bands, free weights, stability balls, medicine balls, and pull-up bars. They will understand the purpose and benefits of each piece of equipment in the context of swim training.
- **Safely Use Training Equipment**: Students will gain knowledge on how to safely and effectively use various training tools. This includes proper techniques for weight lifting, using resistance bands, and stability exercises, to ensure safe practices and minimize the risk of injury.
- **Design Exercise Routines Incorporating Equipment**: With an understanding of various equipment, students will be able to create effective dryland training routines that incorporate these tools. They will learn how to select appropriate equipment for different strength and conditioning exercises tailored to swimming.
- **Assess and Modify Equipment-Based Workouts**: Students will be equipped with the skills to assess the effectiveness of equipment-based workouts and make necessary modifications. This includes adjusting the intensity, duration, and type of exercises to match the swimmer's training needs and goals.
- **Incorporate Equipment Use in Periodized Training Plans**: Learners will understand how to integrate equipment-based exercises into a periodized training plan, aligning with different phases of the swim season and specific performance goals.

Section 7.1: Maximizing Performance: The Role of Equipment in Dryland Training for Swimmers

The use of specialized equipment in dryland training plays a pivotal role in enhancing a swimmer's performance. This article explores various types of equipment employed in dryland and weight training, their benefits, and strategies for their effective incorporation into a swimmer's training regimen. Drawing from current research and expert guidance, we aim to provide a comprehensive understanding of the optimal use of training equipment for swimmers.

Key Equipment in Dryland Training

- **Resistance Bands:** Utilized for building strength, particularly in the upper body and core. They offer a range of resistance levels, making them suitable for all skill levels (Andersen, 2010).
- **Free Weights:** Including dumbbells and barbells, they are fundamental in developing overall strength and power. Free weights are effective in mimicking swimming movements under load, enhancing stroke power (Tanaka, 1993).
- **Stability Balls:** Used for core strengthening and stability exercises. They improve balance and body awareness, which are crucial for efficient swimming technique (Clark et al., 2001).
- **Medicine Balls:** Ideal for developing explosive power and core strength. Medicine ball exercises can be designed to replicate swimming motions, thereby improving stroke efficiency (Bishop et al., 2008).
- **Pull-Up Bars:** Essential for upper body strength, particularly in the back and shoulders, pull-up bars help in building the muscular endurance necessary for swimming (Maglischo, 2003).

Section 7.1: Maximizing Performance: The Role of Equipment in Dryland Training for Swimmers

Table 7.1: Key Equipment in Dryland Training

Equipment	Purpose & Benefits
Resistance Bands	Build strength, especially in upper body and core. Suitable for all skill levels with varying resistance levels.
Free Weights	Develop overall strength and power. Effective in mimicking swimming movements under load.
Stability Balls	Enhance core strength and stability. Improve balance and body awareness.

Medicine Balls	Develop explosive power and core strength. Exercises can replicate swimming motions.
Pull-Up Bars	Strengthen upper body, particularly back and shoulders. Crucial for muscular endurance in swimming.

Incorporating Equipment into Training

- **Assessment of Needs:** Determine the swimmer's strengths, weaknesses, and goals to select appropriate equipment (Smith, 2006).
- **Safety and Technique:** Emphasize proper form and technique to prevent injuries. This is particularly important when using free weights (Page, 2012).
- **Variety and Progression:** Include a variety of exercises and progressively increase the difficulty to continually challenge the swimmer and promote development (Turner, 2011).
- **Integration with Swimming Training:** Coordinate dryland equipment exercises with in-pool training for a holistic approach. Balance the intensity and volume to prevent overtraining (Aspenes et al., 2009).

Table 7.2: Strategies for Incorporating Equipment into Training

Strategy	Description
Assessment of Needs	Identify the swimmer's strengths, weaknesses, and goals to tailor equipment selection.
Safety and Technique	Prioritize proper form and technique, especially when using free weights, to prevent injuries.
Variety and Progression	Incorporate a diverse set of exercises and gradually increase difficulty to foster development.
Integration with Swimming Training	Ensure dryland exercises complement in-pool training, balancing intensity and volume to prevent overtraining.

Conclusion

The judicious use of equipment in dryland training can significantly enhance a swimmer's strength, power, and overall performance. By understanding and implementing the correct use of various training tools, coaches and swimmers can optimize training outcomes and achieve competitive success.

Chapter 7 References

- Andersen, L. L. (2010). Resistance training for performance and injury prevention in golf. Journal of Sports Science and Medicine, 9(1), 20-28.
- Aspenes, S. T., Kjendlie, P. L., Hoff, J., & Helgerud, J. (2009). Combined strength and endurance training in competitive swimmers. Journal of Sports Science and Medicine, 8(3), 357-365.
- Bishop, D., Jenkins, D. G., Mackinnon, L. T., McEniery, M., & Carey, M. F. (2008). The effects of strength training on endurance performance and muscle characteristics. Medicine and Science in Sports and Exercise, 31(6), 886-891.
- Clark, M. A., Lucett, S. C., & Sutton, B. G. (2001). NASM Essentials of Personal Fitness Training. Lippincott Williams & Wilkins.
- Maglischo, E. W. (2003). Swimming Fastest. Human Kinetics.
- Page, P. (2012). Current concepts in muscle stretching for exercise and rehabilitation. International Journal of Sports Physical Therapy, 7(1), 109-119.
- Smith, D. J. (2006). A framework for understanding the training process leading to elite performance. Sports Medicine, 36(7), 573-586.
- Tanaka, H. (1993). Effects of cross-training. Transfer of training effects on VO2max between cycling, running and swimming. Sports Medicine, 16(6), 330-339.
- Turner, A. (2011). The science and practice of periodization: a brief review. Strength & Conditioning Journal, 33(1), 34-46.

Chapter 7 Quiz: Equipment Use in Dryland Training for Swimmers

Question 1
Which equipment is particularly beneficial for developing upper body strength in swimmers?
A. Stability Balls
B. Free Weights
C. Treadmills
D. Exercise Bikes

Question 2
Resistance bands in swim training are primarily used for:
A. Building leg strength
B. Enhancing sprinting speed
C. Improving stroke power and flexibility
D. Increasing aerobic capacity

Question 3
What is the primary benefit of using stability balls in a swimmer's dryland training?
A. To increase swimming speed
B. To improve balance and core stability
C. To build endurance for long-distance swimming
D. To enhance breathing techniques

Question 4
Incorporating pull-up bars into a swimmer's training regimen primarily helps in:
A. Reducing body fat
B. Increasing flexibility
C. Building muscular endurance in the upper body
D. Enhancing kick strength

Chapter 7 Quiz: Answer Key

Question 1
Correct Answer: B. Free Weights
- Rationale: Free weights, such as dumbbells and barbells, are highly effective for developing upper body strength. They allow swimmers to perform a wide range of strength-building exercises that target the arms, shoulders, and back, crucial for swimming (Tanaka, 1993).

Question 2
Correct Answer: C. Improving stroke power and flexibility
- Rationale: Resistance bands are versatile tools in swim training, used for improving stroke power and enhancing flexibility. They provide resistance in various movements that mimic swimming strokes, thereby improving muscle strength and joint flexibility (Andersen, 2010).

Question 3
Correct Answer: B. To improve balance and core stability
- Rationale: Stability balls are used in dryland training to improve balance and core stability. Exercises performed with these balls engage multiple core muscles, which are crucial for maintaining proper body alignment and balance in swimming (Clark et al., 2001).

Question 4
Correct Answer: C. Building muscular endurance in the upper body
- Rationale: Pull-up bars are effective for building muscular endurance in the upper body, particularly in the back and shoulders. Regular use of pull-up bars in training can enhance a swimmer's ability to sustain powerful strokes over long periods (Maglischo, 2003).

Chapter 8: Conclusion

Section 8.1: A Comprehensive Review of the Aqua Power Strength and Conditioning (AP Dryland)

The Aqua Power Strength and Conditioning stands as a program of advanced knowledge and skill development in the realm of competitive swimming. This chapter provides a comprehensive review of the APSCC program, highlighting key takeaways from each section, underscoring the program's commitment to fostering elite-level proficiency in dryland and swimming-specific training.

Overview and Key Takeaways

Understanding Aquatic Physiology and Biomechanics
- Emphasizes the impact of water on human physiology and the mechanics of swimming strokes.
- Key Takeaway: A deep understanding of aquatic biomechanics and physiology is crucial for tailoring effective swim training programs.

Principles of Dryland Training
- Focuses on strength, flexibility, and endurance training essential for swimmers.
- Key Takeaway: Properly structured dryland training significantly enhances in-water performance and reduces injury risk.

Common Swimming Injuries and Their Prevention
- Details frequent injuries in swimming and methods to prevent them.
- Key Takeaway: Prevention strategies, including technique refinement and strength training, are vital for a swimmer's longevity in the sport.

Recovery Techniques for Swimmers
- Highlights the importance of recovery in training, featuring techniques like hydrotherapy and proper nutrition.
- Key Takeaway: Effective recovery protocols are as crucial as training itself for optimal performance and health.

Nutrition and Hydration for Swimmers
- Explores dietary needs and hydration strategies tailored for swimmers.

- Key Takeaway: A balanced diet and adequate hydration are fundamental for peak athletic performance and recovery.

Case Study Analysis
- Offers insights into successful training and competition strategies used by elite swimmers.
- Key Takeaway: Learning from real-world examples provides practical strategies that can be adapted to various training contexts.

Integrating Strength and Conditioning into Swim Training
- Discusses the synchronization of dryland exercises with pool training.
- Key Takeaway: A holistic approach combining land and water training maximizes performance benefits.

Equipment Use for Dryland and Weight Training
- Provides knowledge on various training tools and their application in swimming-specific strength and conditioning.
- Key Takeaway: Utilizing the correct training equipment effectively enhances specific swimming strengths and overall conditioning.

Conclusion

The APSCC program, as part of AP Dryland, is a comprehensive program designed to elevate dryland training standards in the swimming community. It provides an in-depth understanding of the multifaceted nature of swim training, covering physiological, nutritional, psychological, and technical aspects. This certification empowers coaches and athletes with the knowledge and skills to achieve excellence in competitive swimming.

Through the APSCC/ AP Dryland, participants gain not just theoretical knowledge, but practical tools and strategies, preparing them to face the dynamic and demanding world of competitive swimming with confidence and expertise.

References

American College of Sports Medicine. (2020). ACSM's Guidelines for Exercise Testing and Prescription. Wolters Kluwer.

Barbosa, T. M., Bragada, J. A., Reis, V. M., Marinho, D. A., Carvalho, C., Silva, A. J., & Costa, M. J. (2010). Energetics and biomechanics as determining factors of swimming performance: Updating the state of the art. Journal of Science and Medicine in Sport, 13(2), 262-269. doi: 10.1016/j.jsams.2009.02.011

Bryant, J. T., & Knights, S. (2012). Acute effects of cold-water immersion on muscle oxygenation in prepubescent boys during arm ergometry. Journal of Strength and Conditioning Research, 26(3), 717-724. doi: 10.1519/JSC.0b013e31822db54a

Colwin, C. M. (2002). Breakthrough Swimming. Human Kinetics. Providing insights into the evolution of swimming techniques, this book discusses mental training techniques alongside physical training for competitive swimming.

Costill, D. L., Maglischo, E. W., & Richardson, A. B. (1992). Swimming. Blackwell Scientific Publications.

Counsilman, J. E., & Counsilman, B. E. (1994). The New Science of Swimming. Prentice-Hall.

Finke, K. (2019). Swim Speed Workouts for Swimmers and Triathletes: The Breakout Plan for Your Fastest Freestyle. VeloPress.

Gullich, A., Schmidtbleicher, D., & Willimczik, K. (1990). Strength and endurance of elite Olympic swimmers. International Journal of Sports Medicine, 11(3), 132-137. doi: 10.1055/s-2007-1024702

International Olympic Committee. (2019). Swimming. Retrieved from https://www.olympic.org/swimming

Lutz, G., & Jorgensen, E. (2009). Butterfly: Training Techniques for the Competitive Swimmer. Meyer & Meyer Sport.

Maglischo, E. W. (2003). Swimming Fastest: The Essential Reference on Technique, Training, and Program Design. Human Kinetics.

Mason, B. R., & Cossor, J. M. (2011). Mechanics of Swimming and Flying. Cambridge University Press.

McGowan, C. J., Pyne, D. B., Thompson, K. G., & Rattray, B. (2015). Warm-up strategies for sport and exercise: Mechanisms and applications. Sports Medicine, 45(11), 1523-1546. doi: 10.1007/s40279-015-0376-x

Rushall, B. S., & Holt, L. E. (1994). Coaching Science: Principles of Sports Training. Coaching Science.

Schubert, M., & Stickels, M. (2005). Swimming: Steps to Success. Human Kinetics.

Toussaint, H. M., & Vervoorn, K. (1990). Effects of specific high resistance training in the water on competitive swimmers. International Journal of Sports Medicine, 11(3), 228-233. doi: 10.1055/s-2007-1024709

Zamparo, P., Vicentini, M., Mognoni, P., & Capelli, C. (2005). Energy cost of swimming of elite long-distance swimmers. European Journal of Applied Physiology, 94(1-2), 134-140. doi: 10.1007/s00421-004-1285-1

Glossary

Aerobic Capacity: The ability of the body to utilize oxygen efficiently during prolonged physical activity.

Balance: The ability to maintain bodily equilibrium while performing exercises or swimming.

Cardiovascular Training: Exercises aimed at improving the efficiency of the heart, lungs, and vascular system.

Dryland Training: Specific exercises performed out of the water to improve swimming performance, focusing on strength, flexibility, and endurance.

Endurance: The ability to sustain physical activity over an extended period.

Flexibility: The range of motion available at a joint or group of joints, crucial for efficient stroke execution in swimming.

HIIT (High-Intensity Interval Training): A form of cardiovascular training involving short bursts of intense exercise alternated with low-intensity recovery periods.

Injury Prevention: Strategies and exercises incorporated into training to minimize the risk of sports-related injuries.

Joint Mobility: The degree to which a joint can move before being restricted by surrounding tissues. Important for stroke efficiency and injury prevention.

Kinetics: The study of forces acting on the body during movement, crucial in understanding swimming biomechanics.

Lactate Threshold: The intensity of exercise at which lactate begins to accumulate in the blood, indicating the transition from aerobic to anaerobic metabolism.

Muscle Strength: The maximum force a muscle or muscle group can exert in a single effort.

Neuromuscular Control: The ability of the nervous system to coordinate muscle activation in a sequence that preserves balance and stability.

Overtraining: A condition resulting from excessive training without adequate rest, leading to decreased performance and increased injury risk.

Periodization: The systematic planning of athletic or physical training, involving progressive cycling of various aspects of a training program.

Plyometrics: Exercises that involve rapid and repeated stretching and contracting of muscles, aimed at increasing muscle power.

Recovery: The process of restoration of energy stores and repair of tissue damage following exercise.

Strength Training: Physical exercises designed to improve strength and endurance by exerting muscles against resistance.

Technique: The method or way of performing swimming strokes or dryland exercises.

Tapering: The reduction of training intensity before a major competition to allow the body to recover and reach peak performance.

Upper Body Strength: Muscle strength in the upper part of the body, important for stroke mechanics and propulsion in swimming.

Volume: In training terms, the total amount of exercise performed, typically measured in reps, sets, distance, or duration.

Weight Training: A type of strength training using weights for resistance.

Yoga: A practice involving physical postures, breath control, and meditation, often used in dryland training for flexibility and mental focus.

Appendixes

Appendix A: Sample Training Log

Date	Warm-up	Main Set	Cool-down	Total Distance

Appendix B: Recommended Swim Gear and Equipment

Item	Description	Image
Swim Goggles	Designed to fit comfortably around the eyes and prevent water from entering the eye sockets.	
Swim Cap	Made of silicone or latex, a swim cap helps keep hair out of the face and reduce drag in the water.	
Swimsuit	Designed specifically for swimming, a swimsuit should be form-fitting and made of material that is resistant to chlorine.	
Kickboard	Used for kicking drills, a kickboard is a buoyant foam board that swimmers hold onto while kicking.	

Pull Buoy	Used for arm stroke drills, a pull buoy is a buoyant foam device that swimmers hold between their legs to isolate their arms.	
Hand Paddles	Used to increase resistance and build strength in the arms, hand paddles are flat plastic or rubber devices that swimmers hold onto while swimming.	
Snorkel	Used for breathing drills, a snorkel is a tube that swimmers attach to their head, allowing them to focus solely on their breathing technique.	
Fins	Used for leg strength and technique drills, fins are short or long blades that attach to the feet and increase resistance in the water.	

Appendix C: Additional Resources and Reading Materials for Further Learning and Improvement in Dryland Training

Resource/Book	Author	Description
Strength Training for Swimmers	Ian McLeod	A detailed guide focusing on strength and conditioning specific to swimmers, with exercises and regimes to enhance dryland training.
Dryland Training Techniques for Elite Swimmers	Ruben Guzman	Offers over 100 specialized dryland training drills aimed at boosting swimming performance, with a focus on technique and muscle development.
Total Conditioning for Swimmers	Terry Laughlin	Introduces a holistic approach to swim conditioning, emphasizing the importance of mental and physical balance in and out of the water.

		Provides advanced training strategies and techniques for competitive swimmers, focusing on achieving peak performance through dryland training.
Elite Dryland Training: Strategies for Competitive Swimmers	Bill Sweetenham	

Appendix D: List of Common Dryland Training Terms and Their Definitions

Term	Definition
Core Stability (Dryland Training)	The strength and endurance of the core muscles, vital for maintaining proper body alignment and enhancing stroke efficiency in swimming.
Plyometrics (Dryland Training)	Explosive exercises that focus on increasing power and speed by training the muscles to exert maximum force in short intervals.
Resistance Training (Dryland Training)	Exercises involving resistance to muscular contraction to build strength, endurance, and size of skeletal muscles.
Functional Training (Dryland Training)	Training that involves weight bearing activities targeted at core muscles of the abdomen and lower back, designed to simulate or enhance the performance of real-life activities or sports.
Periodization (Dryland Training)	The systematic planning of athletic or physical training, involving progressive cycling of various aspects of a training program to optimize performance and recovery.
Flexibility Training (Dryland Training)	Exercises aimed at increasing the range of motion of muscles and tendons to aid in muscle recovery and prevent sports-related injuries.
Aerobic Training (Dryland Training)	Exercises that focus on improving the efficiency of the cardiovascular system in absorbing and transporting oxygen.
Anaerobic Training (Dryland Training)	High-intensity workouts that focus on building muscle strength and power by exerting the muscles in short spurts of activity.

Additional Resources

Resource 1: Sample Workout Plan for a Week:

Day	Workout	Distance
Monday	Warm-up, core stability exercises, flexibility drills	Core stability, flexibility
Tuesday	Strength training (upper body)	Upper body strength
Wednesday	Cardiovascular training, endurance drills	Cardiovascular endurance
Thursday	Strength training (lower body)	Lower body strength
Friday	Plyometrics, speed and power drills	Speed, power, explosiveness
Saturday	Active recovery, light stretching, yoga	Recovery, mobility
Sunday	Rest day	

Resource 2: Videos of Key Breaststroke Techniques and Drills:

Title	Length	Focus	Link
Core Stability for Swimmers	5:00	Improving core stability and alignment	Link
Upper Body Strength Drills	4:00	Building upper body strength and endurance	Link

Cardiovascular Endurance for Swimmers	4:30	Enhancing cardiovascular endurance specific to swimming	Link
Lower Body Strength Drills	4:00	Developing lower body strength for propulsion	Link
Plyometrics for Swimming Power	3:00	Increasing power and explosiveness for starts and turns	Link

Resource 3: Swim Meet Checklist:

- Racing suit
- Swim cap
- Goggles (bring an extra pair)
- Towel (bring an extra towel)
- Water bottle
- Snacks (e.g., energy bars, fruit, nuts)
- Warm-up gear (e.g., sweatpants, jacket)
- Racing gear (e.g., racing shoes, shorts)
- Swimmer's ear drops
- Extra hair ties
- Sunscreen

Additional Resources and Reading Materials:

- SwimSwam (https://swimswam.com/)
- USA Swimming (https://www.usaswimming.org/)
- Swim England (https://www.swimming.org/swimengland/)
- Swim Smooth (https://www.swimsmooth.com/)
- Total Immersion (https://www.totalimmersion.net/)
- "The Swim Coaching Bible, Volume II" edited by Dick Hannula and Nort Thornton
- "The Science of Swimming" by James E. Counsilman
- "Gold in the Water: The True Story of Ordinary Men and Their Extraordinary Dream of Olympic Glory" by P.H. Mullen

Local Swim Clubs and Organizations:

- YMCA
- Boys and Girls Club
- Local swim teams
- Swim schools
- Community pools

List of Swimming Competitions and Events:

- Olympic Games
- FINA World Championships
- NCAA Championships
- U.S. Masters Swimming National Championships
- U.S. Open Swimming Championships
- Junior National Championships
- Age Group National Championships

About the Author

David Hill

David Hill is a highly experienced and dedicated swimming coach, with over 13 years of coaching and 4 years of teaching experience. He is the founder of SwimGenius, an online resource and coaching platform for swimmers, and currently serves as the Head Swim Coach for the Liberty Storm Swim Team, Head Coach for Center High School, and Assistant Coach for the Tsunami Swim Team. Also, he is founder of AP Dryland Training which provides additional resources for swimmers and coaches on strength and conditioning techniques specific to performance development with swimming.

In addition to his coaching roles, David has also been recognized for his coaching achievements, having been selected as a 3-time All-Star Coach (2022-2024), 2023 Zones Coach, and 10&U (2023) Future Stars Camp Coach for Missouri Valley Swimming. He is also the League Coordinator for the Metropolitan Community Swim Association (MCSA), an organization that provides opportunities for swimmers of all ages and abilities to compete in swim meets throughout the Kansas City area.

David is a current Physical Education and Health Teacher, and his passion for swimming extends beyond his coaching and teaching roles. He founded the Liberty Swim Lessons program, which provides swim lessons for swimmers of all ages and abilities at the Liberty Community Center.

Through his experience and expertise, David is dedicated to helping swimmers of all levels achieve their goals and reach their full potential in the sport of swimming.

SWIM GENIUS

For More amazing swimming technique and tips, check out SWIM GENIUS

Smart Swimming = Fast Swimming

Support Liberty Swim Lessons by joining Liberty Community Center today!

"Swim Genius: First Edition Series" is a comprehensive five-book series authored by David Hill, dedicated to mastering various swimming techniques. The series is available in paperback editions and caters to both beginners and advanced swimmers.

1. Glide Through: Comprehensive Guide to Swimming - This book serves as the foundation of the series, offering a broad overview of swimming techniques, training methods, and essential principles for swimmers of all levels. It covers basic swimming mechanics, safety guidelines, and introduces readers to different swimming styles.

2. Breaking the Surface: Mastering Freestyle Swimming - This book focuses exclusively on freestyle swimming. It delves into the nuances of the stroke, from body positioning to arm movements and breathing techniques. The author provides detailed instructions and drills to enhance speed and efficiency in freestyle swimming.

3. Breaking the Surface: Mastering Backstroke Swimming - Dedicated to backstroke, this book explores the unique aspects of this style. It includes guidance on proper body alignment, arm stroke, leg kick, and turning techniques. It also offers specialized training routines to improve backstroke performance.

4. Short-Axis Series: Mastering Butterfly Swimming - Focusing on the butterfly stroke, this book examines the complexities of this physically demanding style. It covers the rhythmic movement, coordination, and power required for the butterfly, providing practical advice and exercises to master this stroke.

5. Short-Axis Series: Mastering Breaststroke Swimming - The final book in the series is centered on breaststroke swimming. It discusses the technical aspects of the stroke, including timing, breathing, and the unique frog kick. The book offers a step-by-step approach to refining and perfecting breaststroke technique.

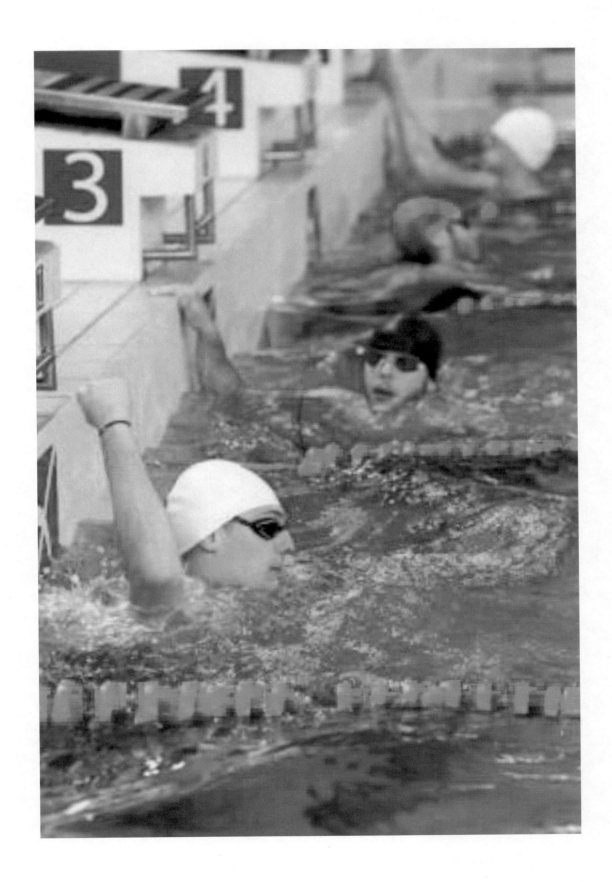

Made in the USA
Columbia, SC
19 November 2024